LADIES DAY

ALANA VALENTINE

CURRENCY PRESS
SYDNEY

GRIFFIN
THEATRE
COMPANY

CURRENT THEATRE SERIES

First published in 2016
by Currency Press Pty Ltd,
PO Box 2287, Strawberry Hills, NSW, 2012, Australia
enquiries@currency.com.au
www.currency.com.au
in association with Griffin Theatre Company

Cataloguing-in-publication data for this title is available from the National
Library of Australia website: www.nla.gov.au

Typeset by Dean Nottle for Currency Press.
Cover image by Brett Boardman; front cover shows Will Harvey.
Cover design by RE:.

Contents

Currency Press acknowledges the Traditional Owners of the Country on which we live and work. We pay our respects to all Aboriginal and Torres Strait Islander Elders, past and present.

Ladies Day is dedicated to the memory of James Waites, who inspired much love, including mine.

Ladies Day was first produced by Griffin Theatre Company at the SBW Stables Theatre, Sydney, on 5 February 2016, with the following cast:

MIKE	Wade Briggs
LIAM	Matthew Backer
LORENA / THERESE / CHORUS 1	Lucia Mastrantone
RODNEY / JOHN / CHORUS 2	Elan Zavelsky

Director, Darren Yap
Set & Costume Designer, James Browne
Lighting Designer, Hugh Hamilton
Sound Designer & Composer, Max Lambert
Associate Composer & Sound Designer, Roger Lock
Stage Manager, Cara Woods

CHARACTERS

MIKE, aka Madame Ovary

LIAM

LORENA

RODNEY

THERESE

JOHN

CHORUS 1

CHORUS 2

Lorena doubles as Therese/Chorus 1
Rodney doubles as John/Chorus 2

SETTING

Broome, Western Australia.

This play went to press before the end of rehearsals and may differ from the play as performed.

SCENE ONE

ALL: [*sung*] The queers in Broome are quite ill-groomed,
       The gays in Broome are fat,
       They've left the sceney city life
       To wear a wide-brimmed hat.
       The queers in Broome are coupled up,
       They renovate and work,
       You might get propositioned by
       The hotel front desk clerk.

      LIAM *and* MIKE *might hold up their phones, connected via FaceTime.*

LIAM: Come.
MIKE: Nah.
LIAM: Why not?
MIKE: Because I'm not in the space to do rural butch drag.
LIAM: It's not compulsory.
MIKE: When is it not?
LIAM: Race day.
MIKE: Please. All those Spode-ugly girls in mass-made frocks.
LIAM: It's fun.
MIKE: All those straight-acting closet types gagging on even saying the word 'cock'.
LIAM: It's not what you think it is.
MIKE: Standing around a denuded dust bowl brushing off clumps of dirt thrown into the air by scrawny horses and hirsute, potato-shaped poofters.
LIAM: That'd be Melbourne, darling. Up here we do glamour, sincerity and friendliness.
MIKE: Chances.
LIAM: Take it.
MIKE: No.
LIAM: Yes.
MIKE: *No!*
LIAM: I'm booking you on a flight.
MIKE: I won't go via Perth.

LIAM: Direct.

MIKE: Club lounge full of mining industry queens cruising for a quickie.

LIAM: How horrible.

MIKE: Business class full of cowboys in prostate-strangling tight pants.

LIAM: And all of them drooling over you.

MIKE: And all of them dazzled by the words 'fresh meat' blinking in neon on my forehead.

LIAM: And what's so wrong with that?

MIKE: I'm off the market, Li. I'm sworn off men, meat and methamphetamine.

> *Pause.*

LIAM: You're right. Don't come.

MIKE: What?

LIAM: Since when did you turn into a lesbian?

MIKE: Some of my best friends are lesbians, Liam.

LIAM: Lesbians don't have best friends, Mike, they have co-dependent refusers of pleasure. They have compliant earnest restricters of fun. Some of your best friends are lesbians, Mike, and you think Broome is dull?

MIKE: They're very broad generalisations, Liam.

LIAM: Just another word for perceptive, my love.

MIKE: When I left John it was my lesbian friends who put me back together.

LIAM: Sure, but they've put you back together as some feral bush pig eco dyke with a sudden love of musky body odour.

MIKE: You're terrible, Laverne.

LIAM: Come.

MIKE: I've got nothing to wear to Ladies Day.

LIAM: We'll find you something, Madame Ovary.

MIKE: Something with a swishy hemline.

LIAM: Done.

SCENE TWO

LORENA: The hardest thing I have ever done, sexually, is when someone has asked me to masturbate for them. Because it's just so private. I mean, they ask so that they can see what to do, how they can please me. And I've done it, it's the hardest thing, because I know I'm going to benefit in the end. But of all the things I've done, and I've done plenty, that's the time I've felt most inhibited. Yeah. I mean getting sex is easy, really. I've gone onto Grindr for some of these guys and I've got them laid in an hour. This friend of mine he was hopeless, dull responses. You know. And I got on there and was just witty and funny and confident and *voilà*. He was having sex within half an hour. And I told him, 'Just don't say anything'. Because he's just not funny, you know. And funny, witty, sweet, that's what people want to see. What you're really like, inside. And the thing is, only some of us can express that. And when we do, it's not always what's really inside. You can learn to be all those things. You can fake those things as easily as a woman can fake an orgasm after a man says, 'Come for me, baby'. 'Oh sure, because you just saying so is going to make me.' Please.

So the second hardest thing I have ever done is this, include myself in my own play. Because I am better at telling other people's stories. At least I'm more comfortable. I know that for every artist it's always about yourself even when it is about someone else, but just for a moment, ignoring the universal theme line and facing the fact that I am putting myself in my own play, this story of a writer who goes to Broome and what happens to her is the second hardest thing I have ever done. Because it is just like the hardest thing I mentioned, just so personal.

Where we really live, what whispers to us, what haunts us, what helps us, what drives us. People can't always talk about that straight out. Can't always put it into words.

And then, just sometimes, you meet someone who can. But not the way you expect.

SCENE THREE

MIKE: You're sure.
LIAM: You will be fine.
MIKE: If you're sure.
LIAM: I'm sure.
MIKE: Alright, I'll do it. I mean, really, what's the worst that can happen?

LIAM: To you? The worst will be if no-one even notices.

MIKE: Well, let's make sure *that* doesn't happen.

> MIKE *spends the scene getting ready—underwear, make-up—the works.*

LIAM: Honestly, Broome is the most tolerant place for homos in Australia. I have never had any trouble at all.

MIKE: Ever worn a dress to Ladies Day?

LIAM: No, but who doesn't love a man in a dress? This is Australia, men in dresses are more popular than the Sydney fish market on Christmas Eve. Any man in any dress will win any competition you care to mount.

MIKE: Yes, well, I'm not caring to mount anyone.

LIAM: Who doesn't love a man in a dress?

MIKE: I've met a few.

LIAM: Not on Ladies Day. People are too excited to care.

MIKE: Until the drink gets into them.

LIAM: Shall I give you the form guide?

MIKE: You're not planning on making an actual bet?

LIAM: Of course I am. But I'm not talking about the horse form guide.

MIKE: No?

LIAM: I'm talking about the gay form guide.

MIKE: Oh, right.

LIAM: Number One: Mr Been Here For Years

> CHORUS 2 *comes out as Number One, appropriately lit and garbed. He parades as if on a catwalk and adopts tableaux poses, both amusing and revealing.*

You'll have to overcome some serious history but there's nothing like an early chat with the honorary gay elder of the Broome scene. Our One considers himself quite the local and he can give you just the opening overview you need.

MIKE: Who's who, who's had who, and who's no longer talking to who.

LIAM: Exactly. He's an absolutely brilliant social butterfly and like many older gay men, both locally and in every regional town, he has no long-term partner but is madly popular with all the heterosexual power couples, most especially the wife whose attention he adores with all the platonic passion you'd ever want mustered.

MIKE: I do love a good daddy figure.

LIAM: Doesn't really do sex, has trouble with real intimacy I think. Gets his kicks from being the linchpin of every party and social gathering.

MIKE: 'Lynch' being the operative word.

LIAM: Absolutely, so play nicely.

MIKE: Comment on the designer shirt.

CHORUS 1 *enters as Ride Number Two.*

LIAM: Ride Number Two: Bad Boy runaway from the big bad scene down south.

MIKE: That's a mouthful.

LIAM: You *wish.* Fit, flirty, fabulous fun. Did drag in his younger days but doesn't anymore, darling. Wants you to have a great time in Broome, wants you to tell everyone it's a great place to have retreated to, but don't ever use the word retreated.

MIKE: Status?

LIAM: Sworn SMMer.

MIKE: Bondage?

LIAM: Serial Married Men.

MIKE: Slip on the old band of gold.

Remaining onstage, CHORUS 2 *puts a shirt back on and dons heels (or a hat).*

LIAM: Ride Number Three: The Sissy Sister.

MIKE: Otherwise known as the competition.

LIAM: Not up here, precious. She'll also be wearing a dress and she will genuinely love having a soul mate to help fly the flag of self-determination and creative do-what-you-wanna-do, be-what-you-wanna-be sisterhood.

MIKE: Just make sure not to steal her thunder.

LIAM: Shake the foundations together. Brew up a little storm of controversy and publicly clutch each other's parts à la Mr Jackson. The punters will love it, the faux trendies will love it, the mayor will love it because it shows what a tolerant haven for the pink dollar we truly are.

MIKE: Until a little kiddie goes missing and suddenly the spotlight is a blowtorch flame.

LIAM: Now don't be bitter.

MIKE: How many years of it being the local church deacon who is the real kiddie fiddler before they don't correlate homo with paedo?

LIAM: It's Ladies Day, Madame Ovary, not the March on Washington.

MIKE: Snatch.

> CHORUS 1 *remains onstage and now transforms to Ride Number Four.*

LIAM: And proud. Ride Four: Straight Acting partner of Sissy Boy who came out late.

MIKE: And still hungry, is my guess.

LIAM: They're talking surrogate babies from Thailand, so no, I don't think there's likely to be a reservation for any fine dining. But he's a real sweetheart, sincere, sorted and very sexy.

MIKE: Oh, you do love them with the whiff of closet mothballs still on them, don't you?

LIAM: In the unlikely event that you feel any kind of little chill wind, and I mean that both literally and metaphorically, Number Four is your big, butch saviour.

MIKE: And you're picturing him grabbing one of the racing nags, galloping past and sweeping you up into his arms now, aren't you?

LIAM: I have two words for you, Mike.

MIKE: Be-have.

LIAM: Free accommodation.

> MIKE, *hat, make-up, lingerie (including suspenders) and shoes in place, now pulls on the frock. He looks* divinely *beautiful. Sexy and gorgeous. This is not eighties drag with bad foundation and a nasty wig—this is glorious, genuinely elegant glamour on a man.*

> MIKE *exits (his transformation may continue offstage).*

SCENE FOUR

LIAM: So I went to a tough school originally, from Year Seven to Year Nine, well not tough, but in a tough area. And I pretty much knew I was gay from a young age, so I didn't have any issue with being who I was, but I got a lot of bullying for it. So it was a big deal for me, and so my parents just moved me out to a private school where everything just changed. I mean the dynamics between different education and wealth had an acceptance around the table. I mean yes, you still have bullying around school, but it was nothing about my orientation. I was open, and in very different areas as well, may we say.

LORENA: So going back to the rough school for a moment…

LIAM: So at that stage I was also dealing with this physical knee joint issue that I have and that was being brought onto it as well. So here's me thinking maybe I'm gay because of my knees. So it was me having to figure out that it doesn't define me, I define myself.

LORENA: But that's a very sophisticated way of thinking. Kids don't really think like that, do they?

LIAM: Oh no, I haven't been able to reflect on that till, well, till now really. Back at that time I thought, 'Well, what am I?'. But I suppose that is that time in youth when you find yourself and I found myself much quicker than other people did. I reckon I knew when I was ten. My sister reckoned she knew when I was two because I preferred to play with Barbie rather than playing with trucks. And like it would always be Barbie. But it's not Barbie anymore.

LORENA: Leave Barbie to me. So you were sent to this new school, Liam.

LIAM: Yeah, and there were a lot of gays in that school who were very aggressive and not nice people. So you had to find yourself within your own friendship group where you could be gay but not be associated with that sort of nastiness. Like there was a hierarchy system and there were a lot of bitchy queens…

LORENA: Like the school was stuffed with them? Like every parent of every gay boy had moved their child there?

LIAM: Yeah, locked behind those private school doors. Can't get in, can't get out.

LORENA: And what's worse than conflict between straights and gays? Conflict between other kinds of gays. So let's move to family? So your mother and father dealt with it and were fine?

LIAM: No, not fine. The way that I came out to my family and friends was obviously not the best way but… I went and got my first STD check and I had a bruise on my arm from where I had my blood taken and I was sixteen and my dad said, 'Why are you doing that?', and I thought I may as well just say it, 'I'm gay'. And then he ran inside and my mum went upstairs, locked the door and didn't come out for three days. Very dramatic.

LORENA: Now we know where you get it from.

LIAM: [*with a laugh*] How do you know me so well?

LORENA: Lifetime in Sydney.

LIAM: And still to this day… like at the time it was hard but it still continues to this day. The denial phase. I live up here with my partner who they refuse to acknowledge, meet, appreciate. So my relationship with them is non-existent. I'm there to say hello, what's going on, besides that it's just not happening. I have got a supportive sister who is much, much older, thirteen-year age gap. Her kids are supportive, met my partner, her husband's parents are supportive so I've got other parents in the mix.

LORENA: Are they aware of the problem with your parents?

LIAM: Everyone knows that I'm a gay person even though my parents think I'm not. Even their friends know but they refuse to acknowledge and discuss it with them. Because they're ashamed.

LORENA: Why do you think they're so hostile?

LIAM: Maybe because of their upbringing, and it's also within their Eastern European background and culture, they don't want to have a negative thing on our family name. Although it's silly. But it's seven years down the track and I have to choose my life over their happiness. And I've had to say, well, I can't… I'll lose somebody else that means more to me than… them.

SCENE FIVE

ALL: [*sung*] The Jigal trees are all in bloom,
  The frangipanis sweet,
  And deep into the sand dunes you
  Can find an active beat.
  The flip-flap slap of rubber thongs,
  Light sweat that's on your skin,
  You drop into your body and
  You drink your senses in.

  MIKE *is struggling with taking off his heels when* RODNEY *enters.*

RODNEY: Well, it's like watching us doctors smoking, isn't it? Or nurses drinking heavily. I mean we know the effects, we *know* intimately what it's doing to our body and still, we do it. Why? Because it feels good, Nagorama, and becaaause everyone else is doing it. I mean I spend all day correcting the damage done by wearing high heels. Not in Broome, in Broome nobody wears high heels on a daily basis, no, the tourists, come up here on their holidays, suddenly they're off their heels and hello lumbar pain. So that's when I see them. If they've been in heels since Adam was a boy they've got bunions and hammer toes and basically they've got deformed feet. So I recommend an intensive treatment regime. I should tell them to stay off the heels for good, but when I used to do that early on they never came back. Gave 'em a case of the guilts and who's gonna pay someone for that privilege? No, I don't tell them how heels reduce the shock absorbing ability of the ankle or how the loss of the inward roll places more stress on the knee, pitching the body forward. Who in perdition wants to hear how the pelvis rotates backwards and that puts strain on the lumbar? *Voilà* instant back pain and welcome to Ladies Day. No, the girls in Broome handle heels like a dog on lino, darling, but no-one is going to see them in flatties on race day and no-one is going to hear me call them out like some kind of chiropractic killjoy.

MIKE: Better than sleeping with a dead policeman, pet.

RODNEY: That's an English expression. Are you English?

MIKE: No, I'm from Sydney.

RODNEY: [*making an indeterminate grunt*] You all get about like that in Sydney, do you?

MIKE: Yeah, well the fashion industry there is doing it tough so the Lord Mayor Clover Moore instituted this city-wide rule that it was compulsory for everyone, men and women, to wear dresses. To support the local designers, you know.

RODNEY: Really?

MIKE: On my life.

> *Pause.*

RODNEY: Well, what do you know? A politician actually doing something to help small business.

MIKE: It's all bike lanes and grosgrain in Sydney these days, pet. It was a natural flow-on from the Mardi Gras parade, you know, to make Sydney the home of couture for men seemed a natural fit.

RODNEY: Not the word I'd use.

MIKE: You don't like it?

RODNEY: I think you look like a pig in lipstick.

MIKE: Says the two a.m. beauty queen.

RODNEY: What does that even mean?

MIKE: It means that you have to wait around till two a.m. till anyone is blind drunk enough to fancy you.

RODNEY: So you're insulting me.

MIKE: I'm doing my best.

Pause.

RODNEY: That's quite funny though, isn't it? You're funny. I don't like you but you're different.

MIKE: Mike. Madame Ovary to my friends.

RODNEY: Rodney. You're not that friend of Liam's?

MIKE: Yeah, do you know Liam?

RODNEY: I'm part of a community group he's trying to set up.

MIKE: So you're friends?

RODNEY: This is Broome, Mike. Those spinifex bushes don't leave much to the imagination.

MIKE: So you're not friends?

RODNEY: Small town. Hard to hide.

MIKE: Oh, he makes you hard?

RODNEY: Have you taken something, Mike?

MIKE: I was looking for the Ladies.

RODNEY: What? To go?

MIKE: No, to lie on the ground and be pissed on from a great height by other women.

RODNEY: That's another joke, right?

MIKE: They call me Trough Man.

RODNEY: They do not.

Pause.

Madame Ovary!

MIKE: That I am.

RODNEY *exits.*

SCENE SIX

LORENA *enters.*

LORENA: So did you have a sense of being gay?

MIKE: Absolutely, but I absolutely never did anything about it. Until I was like nineteen. So.

LORENA: Wow. That's interesting.

MIKE: So the thing is that at school I would never deal… because you know you'd hear, 'That guy, he's gay', or 'She's gay', and the payout that goes on with that. So you're like, 'Oh'. And it's interesting because I was at a party maybe years ago and a guy came up to me and he said, 'What are you doing at this party?', and I go, 'Oh, I'm just looking around…' and he said, 'You bullied me at school!', and I said, 'Really?'. And I don't have any recollection of that at all. I remember him but I don't recollect bullying him. So it took me back, and I dunno, maybe I did, maybe I didn't.

LORENA: Maybe you were just part of a group of people who he felt threatened by?

MIKE: 'Cause I would always stand back when that was happening. Which is the same as bullying really. But you do what you've got to do when that happens.

LORENA: And where was school?

MIKE: Lake Illawarra, which is south of Wollongong.

LORENA: And so you knew there was something about you?

MIKE: I mean in hindsight now I look back and say well of course it was that. If there was a guy and a girl walking in the room I'd be looking at the guy. And I'd fantasise about schoolmates and all that. Of course, you don't know, you struggle with it.

LORENA: Did you name it to yourself?

MIKE: Ah, well, I'm pretty sure I knew. But you also don't know. So I was with women as well but I never had girlfriends.

LORENA: When was your first sexual experience?

MIKE: So my first sexual experience was at sixteen. And that was with a girl and it was very quick and whatever. And I don't think they were very positive experiences for either of us. I mean, they seemed to enjoy the actual sex but, really, what would I know, and it definitely wasn't positive for me. I wasn't really into it. So... definitely I was nine when I had my first relationship, sexual experience with a guy, and it felt amazing. It was a like a relief. Finally.

LORENA: Was that a relationship, not a casual thing?

MIKE: Because I lived in this suburb past Wollongong, it's not a big area and all that. I used to drive to Canberra. Get in my car. Drive to Fyshwick where you can get triple-X gay porn. So I'd buy the porn, drive back, three hours, watch it and be so disgusted I'd throw it away, and then it would all come up in a month's time and I would do it again. Which now... it's just crazy. Just so crazy. But I was throwing it away in disgust because... but that was the only outlet. Gay men now, they grown up with internet, and I think it's changed the way things are. I went overseas, came back, and all of a sudden it was like I met my first... who turned out to be my boyfriend for three years on Yahoo Chat. But you get that experience online that there are other gay people out there.

LORENA: So you went into a long-term relationship straight away?

MIKE: Yep, three years straight up.

SCENE SEVEN

JOHN *is on stage, hammering a horseshoe on an anvil, when* MIKE *enters, adjusting his clothes from his visit to the Ladies.*

JOHN: Wouldn't want to tuck your skirt into your pantyhose.

MIKE: I always thought girls did that deliberately, to show off their arse.

JOHN: Do they?

MIKE: Only I don't think pantyhose is much of a Broome tradition, so they'd have to tuck it into their panties.

JOHN: Well, if you've got an arse like yours, why wouldn't you?

   Pause.

MIKE: You weren't in the form guide.

JOHN: The what?

MIKE: Number Five. Queerboy Cowboy.

JOHN: Queerboy?

MIKE: Oops. My gaydar must have gone down.

   JOHN *gets up, still holding the horseshoe, and comes up to* MIKE *quite close.*

JOHN: Now what would a nice girl like you be doing with a gaydar?

MIKE: I just like to twiddle the dials.

> MIKE *reaches up and runs his fingers through his shirt, around* JOHN*'s nipples.*

JOHN: You move fast.

MIKE: I heard it was race day.

JOHN: Not worried you might scare the horses?

MIKE: I've always found fear a bit of a turn-on.

JOHN: Oh, so you're looking to be turned on, are you?

MIKE: Be hard not to.

JOHN: How hard?

MIKE: Hard as you like.

> JOHN *puts his hand between* MIKE*'s legs.*

JOHN: What's this then?

MIKE: That'd be my riding crop.

JOHN: You're a man.

MIKE: Yes. Is this *The Crying Game*?

JOHN: The what?

MIKE: It's a movie where a heterosexual man doesn't realise his woman is a man.

JOHN: And there are tears before bedtime.

MIKE: Something like that.

> JOHN *is still rubbing* MIKE *between his legs.*

JOHN: What makes you think I'm not a heterosexual man?

MIKE: What makes you think I'm not a woman?

JOHN: Stiff dick.

MIKE: That's my answer too.

> MIKE *is now rubbing between* JOHN*'s legs.*

JOHN: So this is your little *Brokeback Mountain* fantasy, right here.

MIKE: Except Heath Ledger really was straight.

> JOHN *reacts angrily, grabbing* MIKE *aggressively.*

JOHN: You saying I'm not?

MIKE: Easy, cowboy.

JOHN: Thought you liked a bit of fear.

MIKE: I like titillating fear, not actual fear.

JOHN: And what makes you think I do titillating fear?

MIKE: We girls live in hope.

Pause.

JOHN: I'll give you *Brokeback*, and you give me bareback.

MIKE: Can't do that, lover.

JOHN: What?

MIKE: It's safe sex or no sex, pet.

JOHN: You want me to use a condom?

MIKE: I do.

JOHN pulls away and seems to turn for a moment, then suddenly swings back at MIKE, hitting him with the horseshoe.

JOHN: First you call me queer, now you're saying I'm diseased. Is that it? I don't have a faggot bone in my body.

He continues to hit MIKE.

MIKE: Stop. Stop.

JOHN: You wanna wear a dress? You wanna be like a woman. Then you can take it like a woman does.

MIKE: Get away from me.

JOHN: Just like that.

MIKE: Get off me.

JOHN: Simpering, stupid little faggot. I'm nothing like you. I don't take it up the arse. I don't take it up this arse.

He is brutally raping MIKE. He puts his hand over MIKE's face so that he can't scream. When we can hear what MIKE is saying we can hear him saying, 'No, no, no, no'.

JOHN finishes and hits MIKE in the head, sending him unconscious. He gets up.

Next time you be ladylike and make sure your dress is pulled down properly, you hear?

He continues to kick MIKE in the stomach and back. Again and again.

Then he kneels down and begins to cry. A few strangled sobs.

Then he recovers himself and, grabbing one of MIKE's legs, he drags him offstage, leaving a bloodstain as a trail.

SCENE EIGHT

LIAM: I met a guy at work the other day and his son's gay. And the way he spoke about his son was shocking. Like he's quite high in business and he was like, 'Yeah, one of my sons is a faggot and we don't get on because he lives in that gay world'. And I didn't come out to him at all, but it really shocked me because I was like, 'Wow, that's your version of tolerance, huh? And that's your own son.' 'Yeah, we're not very close, he's one of those gays.' One of those gays?

LORENA: So someone said to me, 'No-one comes here to be part of the scene. There's no scene here.' What do you think of that comment?

LIAM: There's a two-way thing to it. During the wet season, when it's quiet, there's about five people on Grindr or something... but during the dry season when the backpackers hit town there's like seventy. So if you mean that sort of scene, that's one thing. But there are a lot of gay people in town who don't want to be part of that but want to be part of a community. And people have been starting to talk about wanting to do something to acknowledge and celebrate that community. So we're going to start an organisation called Pink Broome next year. To address issues, social justice stuff. I think Broome wants to be seen to be welcoming. I think we'll get money out of the council because it's about tourism. Broome is apparently going through a bit of a low economically so they're all convinced that the pink dollar will bring the money in. So I would imagine most people will be supportive, and from what we've received in feedback, most people will be fine. And we will out the ones that don't. So to speak. Retailers will mostly be supportive, there's always an element that won't be supportive and that's... life.

LORENA: Do you know any gay men who work in the mining industry?

LIAM: [*with a laugh*] No.

LORENA: What about the cattle industry?

LIAM: Yes, I know one. But I don't know him. He works on a station. I know somebody that knows of him. But I've never met him. I was just told he was bisexual or something. Well, who isn't bisexual these days?

LORENA: I wonder if working in the cattle industry you call yourself bisexual as a cover?

LIAM: I think it would be pretty hard working in that industry as gay.

When I was meeting teachers and that, living in Fitzroy, they never put a photo up on Grindr and they always used a fake name because they didn't want... because Fitzroy is a small community and they didn't want to come out. But it would also be interesting to look at how supportive the black community is compared to the white community. Whenever I've met Aboriginal elders, and they come to know that I'm gay, nothing is looked at very differently... arms are open in an embrace and they say I'm welcome the same.

LORENA: That's great that's been your experience.

LIAM: Not yours?

LORENA: Well, my experience is not really relevant. You'd have to ask Aboriginal gay and lesbian people.

LIAM: I think what I was saying with the teachers is also in the nursing community and the police. I mean it's his own fear as well, but there's quite a few like that that don't want to come out in that sense. It's a very blokey world, the cattle world. But I had an experience... There was this butcher from Yeeda, and I was at the races when he first came, and he was saying, 'He's a faggot, he's a faggot', until this big-shot cattleman went over and said, 'Hey, what are you doing, that's not acceptable'. Yeah, and then he decides to be nice after that.

LORENA: Just nice enough so that he can ask you, 'Yeah, but which one is the girl?'

LIAM: So true.

LORENA: You know when you've got one that's just a little bit too inter-ested in strict gender roles. I've met...

LIAM: But station workers are quite tight-knit crews. So it would be a tough place to have to come out.

LORENA: It's like coming out in a football team or something. It's about more than you, in a sense.

LIAM: Yep.

SCENE NINE

MIKE *is badly injured, semi-conscious.* LIAM *and* RODNEY *are leaning over him.*

LIAM: Mike?

MIKE: [*in a whisper*] Catch him?

LIAM: Catch who?

MIKE: Get him?

LIAM: The doctor is here, Mike.

RODNEY: Mike, can you hear me?

LIAM: The ambulance is coming.

MIKE: Catch him.

LIAM: He's talking about catching someone.

RODNEY: He may not know what he's saying.

LIAM: Mike, have you been kicked by a horse?

MIKE: Giraffe.

RODNEY: Mike, you've been kicked by a horse.

MIKE: He hurt me, Liam, he hurt me so much.

RODNEY: He should stop trying to speak.

LIAM: Why would he have gone into the stable?

MIKE: Catch the stunt man.

LIAM: What?

MIKE: Match the front plan.

RODNEY: He's not making sense.

MIKE: [*almost crying*] Patch the punch bag.

LIAM: You'll examine him?

RODNEY: When he gets to the hospital. They'll examine him there.

LIAM: They'll examine you at the hospital, Mike. We think you've been
    kicked by a horse.

MIKE: Scratch the lounge chair.

LIAM: Yep, okay. Just rest now.

RODNEY: Why is he in a dress?

LIAM: Excuse me?

RODNEY: Why is he wearing a dress?

LIAM: Are you really asking me that?

RODNEY: It's not important.

LIAM: Well, I don't know. Is it medically relevant?

    Pause.

    Are you a homophobe, Rodney?

RODNEY: Can you be a gay homophobe?

LIAM: Of course you can.

RODNEY: Listen, your friend can say odd things because he's been kicked by a horse. What's your excuse?

MIKE: Catch the cowboy.

LIAM: Let's see when I post it.

RODNEY: Why would you do that?

LIAM: Doctor asks for fashion report while treating injured man.

RODNEY: Liam, you're upset.

LIAM: How does it threaten you, though? I mean really, how does what he wears have anything to do with anything?

Pause.

RODNEY: Look, I just asked, alright? It was an innocent enquiry. It is unusual.

LIAM: No, it's discriminatory.

RODNEY: Fine. I apologise.

LIAM: How long do you think it will be?

RODNEY: Soon, I hope. But there'll be traffic because of the races.

LIAM: But they'll let the emergency vehicles through?

RODNEY: If they can.

MIKE: Why is the shoe man here?

LIAM: Have you met?

RODNEY: Briefly.

LIAM: He's a doctor, Mike.

MIKE: He was stronger than me, I fought but he was so much stronger.

RODNEY: You've been kicked by a horse.

MIKE: I've been kicked by a horse.

RODNEY: There. What did I tell you?

LIAM: He was just repeating what you said.

MIKE: He likes my dress.

Pause.

RODNEY: Sure.

LIAM: He's afraid of being labelled a bigot.

MIKE: But not of being one.

RODNEY: People do get unfairly accused, you know.

LIAM: I can't believe this has all become about you.

MIKE: Where's the ambulance?

SCENE TEN

LORENA: [*sung*] A chance encounter by the pool,
        The story of his life.
        He wore a dress to Ladies Day
        And paid a nasty price.
        His truth is often brutal
        And difficult to say
        But when he tells his story
        She cannot look away.
MIKE: It's not like you think.
LIAM: What isn't?
MIKE: Being raped.
LIAM: It's good that you're ready to talk about this.
MIKE: I want to, the trouble is, no-one else does.
LIAM: No-one else who?
MIKE: I want to talk about how you leave your body after it.
LIAM: What do you mean leave your body?
MIKE: I mean, whereas once you had the illusion that you and your body were the same thing, suddenly you realise that your body is separate from you. That's the worst thing about being raped. Suddenly you're not in your body anymore.
LIAM: Well, where are you?
MIKE: Out of it.
LIAM: You mean because of the physical pain?
MIKE: Yeah and I'll deal with that any way I hipping want to.
LIAM: What?
MIKE: What?
LIAM: You said hipping.
MIKE: What does hipping mean?
LIAM: I don't know, that's why I asked you.
MIKE: Stop picking on me.
LIAM: I'm not!
MIKE: There's brain damage, isn't there?

    THERESE *enters. She is wearing a police uniform, or a police badge.*

THERESE: Is there?

LIAM: Mike, this is Therese.

MIKE: Are you family?

THERESE: He doesn't recognise people?

LIAM: No, he does.

MIKE: Because you look like family.

THERESE: Is it a kind of amnesia?

LIAM: No, it's a kind of irritating tic really.

MIKE: Maybe bi-curious.

THERESE: Oh. Family as in homosexual.

LIAM: That's right.

MIKE: I mean, I know I was bleary, but even I don't think family means biology. Please. I was raped, not lobotomised.

THERESE: Were you raped?

LIAM: Does he need to give a statement?

THERESE: Yes. As long as halfway through he doesn't say the experience is surreal or that he feels like he is stuck in a bad TV crime movie or that he just wants to forget about it after all.

MIKE: Told you she was family. Easily bored with the mundane details of reality. You must struggle with the procedural nature of your work.

THERESE: Not really. I struggle with the tyranny of distance.

LIAM: Big areas, few police.

THERESE: Can we start with a description?

MIKE: Oh, he was gorgeous. Built. Fit. Hung.

THERESE: You wanted to have sex with him?

MIKE: You bet your life I did.

THERESE: So it was consensual?

MIKE: At first.

> *Pause.*

THERESE: Yeah, see, 'at first' is a blurry line.

MIKE: I wanted to have sex with him, girlfriend, not be bashed and raped. [*To* LIAM] What are you playing at, bringing me some uptight dyke who tells me that 'at first is a blurry line'.

THERESE: I'm going to let that go because he's in shock.

MIKE: What, you don't like being called an uptight dyke? I haven't even started on the omissions in your depilatory regime, nor the massive lapses in your style sensibility. If you think being called an uptight dyke is tough, try being called a festering eyesore, a slovenly crank or a frumpy lump of a dumped-out-in-Broome cunt.

THERESE: [*to* LIAM] You said he'd be challenging to help.

LIAM: Yeah. He's still really upset.

THERESE: He's a pretty standard bile-filled queen.

Pause.

MIKE: Who are you calling standard, girl?

THERESE: The real problem is not his mouth, it's identification. If you could get a description from him…

LIAM: He can draw.

THERESE: Great. Bring it down to the station. I'll take it from there.

She exits.

MIKE: Nice girl.

LIAM: Yeah.

MIKE: Does she have a partner?

LIAM: Not that I know of.

MIKE: Might be fun to help her with that.

SCENE ELEVEN

LORENA: [*sung*] He meets her in the morning and
      They have a drink at night,
      He tells her the whole story,
      Recreates the tension right,
      And as he tells the moments he
      Can feel his horror ease,
      As if the act of telling it can
      Numb it and relieve.

Liam's house. On the walls are crayon drawings of the face of the attacker.

LIAM: Mike?

There is no answer from MIKE, *who is lying, out of it, on a sofa.*

Mike?

MIKE: What?

LIAM: What are you doing?

MIKE: You told me to rest.

LIAM: Are you high?

MIKE: You said to do a drawing of him.

LIAM: Not on the wall, on a sheet of paper.

MIKE: Oops.

LIAM: Mike.

MIKE: …

LIAM: Mike!

MIKE: What?

LIAM: What are you doing?

MIKE: I'm relaxing. I'm resting. I'm recovering. I'm using every word that ever started with the letter 'r'. Hang on. I'm auditioning for 'Sesame Street'. Do we have that in Australia still? Do you get it in Broome?

LIAM: I think we might need to get you some help, Mike.

MIKE: That's why I did the drawing.

LIAM: On a piece of paper.

MIKE: I did it alright. I did it where and when I could.

LIAM: Alright.

Pause.

MIKE: I couldn't find any paper. This way you can take a screen shot of it.

LIAM: What are you doing?

MIKE: I'm struggling.

LIAM: You're self-medicating.

MIKE: I'm taking drugs. I've always taken drugs. Now I'm taking prescription drugs provided by my doctor.

LIAM: Do you think you could talk to a counsellor?

MIKE: After it happened I was inappropriately rational. Now I'm inappropriately irrational. When am I going to get with the rule book and be appropriately appropriate at the appropriate appropriation?

LIAM: Now you're playing the victim.

MIKE: I am the victim. And where's the perpetrator? Getting on with his life, accusation free.

LIAM: If I arranged for you to see someone, I bet it could help.

MIKE: So take a screen shot, send it to whoever you like!

LIAM: Stop yelling at me.

MIKE: I hate you. I hate you for coming in here and hassling me.

LIAM: I know.

MIKE: I hate you, I hate him, and most of all I hate, hate, hate myself.

LIAM: I know.

MIKE: You said I would be alright.

LIAM: I know.

MIKE: You should have known. Someone should have known. Someone should have warned me.

LIAM: Yeah. Life should be a bowl of cherries.

MIKE: Yes.

> MIKE *collapses on the floor, furious, then crying.*

LIAM: Maybe if we went out for a while.

MIKE: No.

LIAM: Just to the beach.

MIKE: Too open.

LIAM: What?

MIKE: It's too open. I don't like open spaces.

LIAM: Why not?

MIKE: Do I have to do that too? Do I have to work out why not? I just don't, okay? I just don't. I like to be inside, tight, against the wall, protected. That's all I know. Alright?

LIAM: Alright.

> *He goes to the wall and takes a photo of the drawing on his phone.*

Will I leave this here or clean it off?

MIKE: Either way. It's not like cleaning it off is going to make him go away.

> LIAM *goes over to* MIKE. *He puts his arms out to give him a hug.*

Don't. There has to be another way that you can help me to exorcise him.

> LIAM *stands with his arms outstretched.*

SCENE TWELVE

RODNEY: [*sung*] The queers in Broome are now in tune,
       With business on the brink,
       They've got a plan, rebrand the town,
       Attract the dollar pink.

> They'll take their wigs out for a show
> And make a queerboy pitch,
> Selling Broome as homo-friendly,
> Needs to go without a hitch.

LIAM *enters carrying a pink broom.*

RODNEY: What's that?

LIAM: It's a pink broom.

RODNEY: I can see it's a pink broom, Glinda, what's it for?

LIAM: It's a symbol of gay pride.

RODNEY: It's not a symbol of gay pride. It's a symbol of… Halloween for dyke witches of the west.

LIAM: Rodney, there are some lesbians in Broome, you know.

RODNEY: Yes, but who cares?

LIAM: Rodney!

RODNEY: I mean, if every lesbian in Australia came to Broome and buried themselves headfirst in the salt hills of Port Hedland, who would care?

LIAM: Presumably the miners left with lemon-flavoured salt hills.

RODNEY *laughs.*

RODNEY: Don't encourage me.

LIAM: You're just so old school. I don't know how we're going to change you.

RODNEY: Gay men and lesbians are both homosexual like sane men and lunatics are both homo sapiens.

LIAM: You're a stupid misogynist.

RODNEY: I have a PhD.

LIAM: In the ancient history of dreary old queens. Well, what do you suggest as a symbol of gay pride?

RODNEY: I don't know. A pink broomstick up the arse of yours truly?

LIAM: And that's the kind of implied violence that's got me thinking that Pink Broome should start to talk about this stuff.

RODNEY: Oh, lighten up. I don't want to rally around some flea-bitten scruff of dyed straw, that's all.

LIAM: You don't want to face what this town is really like either. A broomstick up the arse is hardly a neutral comment. Sexual violence does happen here.

RODNEY: I don't want to pretend it doesn't happen. Of course I know it happens. It's just not usual. It's actually unusual. In fact, I've never heard of it ever, in my whole time here. So it's not so much unusual, as… unheard of. Freakish.

LIAM: Well, I'm going to talk about it if I'm asked.

RODNEY: Asked?

LIAM: This writer, Lorena. I think Mike wants to talk about it too.

RODNEY: About what?

LIAM: About sexual violence and gay men.

RODNEY: And that's what you want Broome to be known for?

LIAM: No, but it does happen here.

RODNEY: And how quickly will down-southers jump to say it's a backwater?

LIAM: Very quickly.

RODNEY: And do you want to help them along, do you?

LIAM: No.

RODNEY: That's what they want to paste onto this place. That's how they want to keep seeing us. As bigoted, frontier rapists when there are just as many—more—many, many more assaults in those capital cities than up here. In Melbourne I'm scared to walk down the streets at night. Up here, I'm laughing.

LIAM: Yeah, but Mike says this could be an opportunity to start the conversation.

RODNEY: Mike is talking to her?

LIAM: Yes.

RODNEY: About what?

LIAM: Mike is working through some things.

Pause.

RODNEY: Can I ask you a personal question?

LIAM: Not really.

Long pause.

What?

RODNEY: Are you in love with Mike?

LIAM: I love him. As a friend.

RODNEY: Have you ever asked yourself?

LIAM: He's my friend.

RODNEY: Are you sure?

LIAM: Yes.

RODNEY: How sure?

LIAM: He's been my friend for a long time.

RODNEY: Feelings can change.

LIAM: They haven't.

RODNEY: Sure?

LIAM: Yes.

RODNEY: You can't tell him?

LIAM: I don't love him. Not like that.

RODNEY: And this would be the worst possible time. The worst possible moment. To admit it.

LIAM: You don't know me well enough to say that, Rodney.

RODNEY: He'd feel betrayed.

LIAM: Boy, you are a dog with a bone.

RODNEY: And what he doesn't need right now is to feel betrayed by his best friend admitting that he has feelings for him. Sexual feelings for him.

LIAM: I'm warning you, Rodney. Mind your own business.

RODNEY: Wanting to kiss him, wanting to touch him.

LIAM: I said stop it.

>   *Pause.*

RODNEY: Swear you're not in love with him.

LIAM: I swear.

RODNEY: Say it.

LIAM: No.

RODNEY: What am I going to do? Tell him? He's not going to listen to me.

LIAM: I'm not listening to you.

RODNEY: Liam, say it aloud. You've been hiding it all this time, since when?

LIAM: Why are you doing this?

RODNEY: When he's not around, you miss him, when he is around, you're alive, like you never feel when he's not around. And whatever he's going through there's the tiniest, tiniest part of you that's happy that he's at least still here, and you will do just about anything to keep him here.

SCENE THIRTEEN

LIAM: [*sung*] The men in Broome are proudly camp,
      They don't eschew the sissy stamp,
      They dragon boat race in a wig,
      They couldn't give a flying fig.
RODNEY: With so much fun and so much flair,
      It's criminal to fuel despair,
      And maybe love is on the breeze,
      Just the thing to pretty please.
LORENA: So, gay men in Broome.
RODNEY: Broome is incredibly tolerant.
LORENA: That's what everyone is telling me.

    Pause.

RODNEY: Why did you come here?
LORENA: I came here on holiday.
RODNEY: So why are you interviewing people?
LORENA: I'm just… It seems like an interesting place.
RODNEY: An interesting place! What the hell is that?
LORENA: An invisible place. A voiceless place.
RODNEY: I don't think so.
LORENA: I've heard a story.
RODNEY: From whom?
LORENA: I heard a story about how Broome is not so tolerant.
RODNEY: And one story makes the town intolerant, does it?
LORENA: Can we just cool this down a little?
RODNEY: Don't portray Broome as bigoted. Because it's not.
LORENA: There are bigots everywhere. There are incidents everywhere.
   Including Broome.
RODNEY: Why are you digging?
LORENA: Who says I am?
RODNEY: Well, no-one has ever said anything to me.
LORENA: Well, you're not me.
RODNEY: What does that mean?
LORENA: I mean, I'm good at this.
RODNEY: Good at what?

LORENA: I'm a good listener.

RODNEY: So people tell you things they don't say to anyone else?

LORENA: Which is important, isn't it?

RODNEY: You're like a snake charmer. You charm stories out of people and before they know it they're telling you stuff they've never told anyone and it does them no good to dwell on.

LORENA: Says you.

RODNEY: Everyone says it's tolerant and suddenly you're suspicious.

LORENA: I think it depends on who you ask.

RODNEY: People are going to want to impress you.

LORENA: You don't want to impress me.

> *Pause.*

RODNEY: Are you going to show all the people who have a good time at the races? The faggots who walk around with their hairdos and tight-fitting pants and everyone loves them. Are you going to show that?

LORENA: Yes.

RODNEY: But…

LORENA: But there's got to be room for the ugly truth.

RODNEY: Whose ugly truth?

LORENA: I have confidentiality issues. If I include some stories it will be anonymously.

RODNEY: What gives you the right to include it at all?

LORENA: This man's attacker hasn't been found. It's set off a full reaction in him and brought up abuse from his past.

RODNEY: Whoa, whoa whoa whoa whoa.

LORENA: What?

RODNEY: The abuse from his past.

LORENA: That's what he's said.

RODNEY: So now we became gay because we're abused, is that the story?

LORENA: There are gay men who were abused as children.

RODNEY: But not all gay men.

LORENA: Not you, for instance.

RODNEY: Not me.

LORENA: So tell me your story, what concerns you at the moment?

RODNEY: Why should I?

LORENA: Tell me about you.

RODNEY: I don't think so.

LORENA: Then tell me about Broome. About the Broome you love.

Pause.

RODNEY: It's interesting that transition that I think every gay man makes from when you're young and you know that you have beauty and you know how to use it. And you do know. And when you're younger and you have that extraordinary power you're so conscious of your ability to turn it on, withhold it, offer it. Like outwardly... even inwardly... you can have a vexed relationship to it and sort of perform a kind of overcompensation, you know, 'Don't treat me like I'm just beautiful', but in hindsight even that underlines your beauty because ugly people don't get to be like, 'Don't treat me like I'm just beautiful'. I mean, I have landed very beautiful partners by deliberately, manipulatively ignoring their beauty and playing to their intelligence. It's just too easy. And when you've got it... if it gets you an extra martini you're not going to say no. Because, frankly, it's just more expensive once you start to lose it. Like people have said to me, 'Didn't you find Sydney expensive?' And I was like, 'Don't be ridiculous... I didn't buy any drinks for myself in my twenties'. I mean, I had no idea how much my vodka martini habit was costing other people. It's a real currency.

But there's not long before you develop the fear of losing it. Much sooner than you think you're going... Hey, I know I'm not sixteen anymore... So the fear of losing it starts long before you do actually lose it. That moment when you walk into a room and you suddenly know you are not the most beautiful person in it. If you're gay you know where you sit in the hierarchy, my God, do you know. If you're straight and you've never had it you watch the people who have it pretend that they don't. But if you're gay nobody pretends that they don't have it. They just ruthlessly work their place in the hierarchy.

I remember being young and gay and pretty in Sydney and I can literally remember at the age of twenty-nine it just changed. And for it to last till twenty-nine... that was a long run, darling. Growing up I was tall and skinny and I hated it and felt like I needed to be muscley and manly and I tried to grow a beard and work out at the gym, to no avail. And then I walked into a gay bar and being tall and skinny was attractive to a lot of people. A lot of people. But now, that's gone, and I'm probably not attractive to anyone in the room. You do know when it's gone and, well, I just didn't cope with it. I tried to. I tried to transition but all around me there were people saying, 'Well yeah, once it goes, life as you know it is basically over'. Seriously. People who told me that they just never went out anymore because they couldn't handle the change. And yeah, that's when I moved to Broome. It was move or, well... I guess I can say it. Move or you know... not live. As in... Yes. I can't say it. But. I dunno. Maybe you think that's terribly superficial.

In some ways I'm a bit of a... I love people but I'm a bit of a loner now. Not a loner, but I find intimacy a little bit hard, it's stressful for me, it really is. It's stressful... I get butterflies... Sometimes I think I'm not really good at sex anymore, but then I think that's a bit of a cop-out. No, I do get nervous about it so it's nearly too hard. And I've found I can look after myself, I certainly can't look after anyone else.

When I was in Sydney I used to go to the opening of new night-clubs and fashion stores. When I came to Broome I've found myself going to the opening of Chicken Treat and Red Rooster. So it's on a much smaller scale, but the same thing happens! Kiss kiss, hello darling, work the crowd, work the room. So I came here to get away from a busy social life but unfortunately it follows you if you've got that kind of nature.

I certainly want everyone to like me. I do want people to like me. I like a little bit of a lot of people. So I find that about two hours is about the right amount of time with any one person.

An intimacy with a lot of people is easy. But with one... I would really freeze up. And then silent patches in conversation does my head in... I worry... so that I end up saying something that fills in that gap and it sometimes can be a bit silly... you know... but then what happens... the people that I'm attracted to don't want the talk because they're happy with not saying a word... so it really blows it... because I'm Mister Chatty and worried about the pregnant pauses. I have found people who I'm really attracted to, but my Hollywood side... my fliberty gibbert, annoys them in the end. Because I like the social side, the people I'm attracted to usually just want the one on one.

SCENE FOURTEEN

Liam's house.

MIKE: I'm thinking of going back.
LIAM: When?
MIKE: Soon.
LIAM: Yeah.
MIKE: I'm not improving. This is not helping.
LIAM: It still might.
MIKE: You have more faith in me than I have in myself.
LIAM: I hold onto it when you put it down every now and then.
MIKE: You've always done that for me, haven't you, Lee?

> *Pause.*

LIAM: When will you go?
MIKE: You trying to get rid of me?
LIAM: No.
MIKE: Ask me and I'll stay.

> *Pause.*

LIAM: If you need to go back then you should go.
MIKE: Right.
LIAM: I'm sorry it turned out like this.
MIKE: Us. This?

> *Pause.*

LIAM: We'll still be friends.
MIKE: Is that what we are?
LIAM: What else can we be? Right now.

> *Pause.*

MIKE: Come here.

> LIAM *goes over to him.*

I can't kiss you.
LIAM: No.
MIKE: But you can come close.

> MIKE *touches* LIAM*'s face gently with his own, sliding his cheek along his face. Their bodies* do not *touch, nor do their mouths.*

LIAM: What can I do?

MIKE: Watch me.

> MIKE *puts his hand down his pants and begins to touch himself.* LIAM *watches him as he begins to masturbate. But then* MIKE *stops, terribly frustrated.*

I can't.

LIAM: Let me.

MIKE: No.

LIAM: Please.

> LIAM *moves toward him.*

> MIKE *becomes almost unhinged.*

MIKE: No! No! I said don't touch me.

LIAM: Alright.

MIKE: Don't touch me. Don't touch me. Get away from me!

> *Pause.*

I'm sorry. I'm sorry. I'm sorry.

> LIAM *moves to the other side of the stage, collapsed in a crouched heap.*

Liam.

LIAM: What?

MIKE: Don't hate me.

LIAM: I don't hate you, Mike. I love you.

MIKE: Why?

LIAM: …

MIKE: I mean, why now?

LIAM: I don't know.

MIKE: You think you can save me. You think you can heal me.

LIAM: No.

MIKE: Then why?

LIAM: Why wouldn't someone be able to love you?

> *Pause.*

MIKE: Not still.

LIAM: Yes, still.

MIKE: Not me.

Pause.

LIAM: Let's go diving. Come on. No words, so no misunderstanding.

MIKE: That's alright.

LIAM: Come on, let's do one incredible thing so that this trip isn't all bad memories.

MIKE: Alright.

LIAM: You'll come?

MIKE: I don't have any gear.

LIAM: We'll hire it.

MIKE: Okay.

LIAM: Great. And, Mike, I'm sorry.

MIKE: That's alright.

LIAM: I presumed.

MIKE: You did.

LIAM: I thought you were feeling something too.

MIKE: You were mistaken.

SCENE FIFTEEN

An underwater diving scene. With video or theatrical tricks to represent the two of them diving on a coral reef. Install a glass tank, by all means.

SCENE SIXTEEN

They are having a drink.

MIKE: What I loved most is that you can't talk.

LIAM: Most?

MIKE: Yes, most. You keep wanting to talk and comment but you can't, you're locked in your own little world.

LIAM: You're in their world, is the way I put it.

MIKE: And the colours. It's a riot, a pageant... it puts paid to Victor Hugo.

LIAM: Who?

MIKE: You've heard of Victor Hugo.

LIAM: Sorry.

MIKE: He wrote *Les Misérables*.

LIAM: Great. And does *Les Misérables* have a scene set underwater?

MIKE: No, Victor Hugo said, 'Everything being a constant...

Pause.

'… there is no…

Pause.

'… left'. But there is, it's just underwater.

LIAM: There is no… what?

MIKE: Well, what do you think would fit in that sentence?

LIAM: I don't know.

MIKE: A riot, a pageant, a…

LIAM: Colourful place.

MIKE: A place with rides and clowns and fairy floss.

LIAM: A fair?

MIKE: Are you asking again?

LIAM: No. An amusement park.

MIKE: What's another word for that?

LIAM: I don't know.

MIKE: What did you drive here in?

LIAM: A car.

MIKE: And what joins the top half of your leg to the bottom?

LIAM: A joint.

MIKE: Which joint?

LIAM: A ball joint.

MIKE: No, what do you call it? A doctor hits it with a hammer to test your reflexes.

LIAM: Your knee.

MIKE: So put that together.

LIAM: Car, knee.

MIKE: What stops air coming out of your inner tube?

LIAM: I don't have an inner tube.

MIKE: On your bicycle, you crank.

LIAM: I don't have a bicycle.

MIKE: Well, you should get one. They're good exercise and good for the environment.

LIAM: I don't care about the environment.

MIKE: The thing that stops the air.

LIAM: …

MIKE: Metal. You screw it on.

LIAM: Valve.

MIKE: Just the first letters.

LIAM: Car, knee, val.

MIKE: So what is it?

LIAM: Car, knee, val.

MIKE: Yes?

LIAM: Car, knee, vor?

MIKE: No, you had it.

LIAM: Car, knee, val.

MIKE: You're saying it.

LIAM: What?

MIKE: What? A pageant, an amusement park…

LIAM: I don't know.

MIKE: 'Everything being a constant…

> *Pause.*

'… there is no…

> *Pause.*

'… left'.

LIAM: Tell me.

MIKE: No.

LIAM: Everything being a constant pain, there is no pain left.

MIKE: No.

LIAM: Tell me.

MIKE: Say it again.

LIAM: Car, knee, val.

MIKE: I thought you were smart.

LIAM: I am smart.

MIKE: No, you're not.

LIAM: Car, knee, val. Oh. Carnival.

MIKE: The penny drops.

LIAM: Carnival. You needed to give me 'varl' instead of 'val'.

MIKE: I needed to give you a brain transplant.

LIAM: I got it. Eventually.

MIKE: Everything being a constant carnival, there is no carnival left.

LIAM: And is he talking about the internet?

> *They are screaming with laughter by now.*

MIKE: No, he's Victor Hugo, he died before the internet happened.

LIAM: That's bad. For him.

MIKE: He's acclaimed as one of France's greatest writers.

LIAM: Yes, but he's dead.

MIKE: And you're insane.

LIAM: And that's what you're saying: that there is a carnival left, it's just underwater.

MIKE: Well yes, I was trying to say that about three years ago.

LIAM: No need to be rude.

MIKE: Did you really not know or were you doing it deliberately?

LIAM: I really didn't know. But I would have done it deliberately to make you laugh like that.

> MIKE *exits.*

> > [*Sung*] I can't breathe for thinking about your mouth,
> > Can't see, recalling your surly pout
> > In the perfume of you I long to douse,
> > I can't breathe for thinking about your mouth.
> >
> > I can't sleep for dreaming about your skin,
> > The ache of longing, you've put me in,
> > My fingers run gently along your chin,
> > I can't sleep for dreaming about your skin.
> >
> > 'Cause I'm just this side of the line you drew,
> > But my mind keeps wandering over,
> > Revealing, concealing myself from you,
> > Dizzy with anticipation.

SCENE SEVENTEEN

MIKE: So they give me this counsellor and I immediately know we're not going to get along because what is she wearing?

Polyester.

And not designer polyester, though even putting those two words together is an oxymoron in my books, but this, ladies, is polyester, made in China.

I mean, I'm not being difficult, or sarcastic.

I'm deadly serious.

How am I supposed to listen to someone like that, let alone respect them?

It's forty-one degrees and she's in polyester.

And I've got mental health problems?

Friends.

So she asks me, 'What really makes you happy when you're really down?'

And I say, 'When I don't know what to choose, I choose a beautiful dress', and she laughs.

She actually laughs.

And then she says, 'Do you think your interest in dresses is a way of loathing yourself as a man?', and I say, 'Dresses are not bad for men. Air around the groin, delicate fabrics on the skin, discovery of the undiscovered waist—can all be new experiences for some men.'

And then she tells me that I should stop comparing myself to others and live my own dreams and that no-one is my enemy except myself.

No-one is my enemy except myself.

To a man who has been sexually assaulted.

I said, lady, my life changed the day I realised that I had been dressing down to please other people.

When I realised that the universe wanted me to enjoy luxury fabrics.

And you, sweetness, will get some pride when you *start* comparing yourself to others and take some interest in putting them to shame.

When you realise that other people's opinions do matter and that you cannot simply impress the pants off them but intimidate the hell out of them.

Happiness, my little polyester-swathed frump, is the day you realise life is about winning and losing and losing involves foundation that does not have a sunscreen component and winning, my pathetically dowdy little friend, involves a silk linen blazer with mother of pearl details.

Well, she burst into tears.

And so did I.

It was all very cathartic.

And then she told me that she'd become a counsellor because of her own struggles with self-esteem, that her mother had always criticised her weight and dressed her in loose clothing even as a child, so that she grew up with huge body image issues.

Poor petal.

And then she told me that her mother wouldn't even let her use tampons because she said it was going to take her virginity, so the poor woman was forced to use those hideous surfboard-like pads all her life, apparently until very recently.

And then she told me that that is really common among her Asian clients—don't go all weird on me, there are a lot of Asian/Australians in Broome, okay, so she used the word 'Asian clients'—she told me that recently one of her Asian clients actually asked her not only how to insert a tampon but then asked her to actually show her, like go into the toilet and show her how she inserted it into herself. That, my darling, I said, that is real commitment to your work. And another client, if you can believe it, honestly thought that women urinated out of the same place that they menstruate.

And I said, 'Do you mean she's never put her hand down there to check?'

And we both howled with laughter.

She was crying with laughter.

And I don't have a vast knowledge of female anatomy, friends, but even I know that the urethra is separate from the vagina.

She was all pity and poor little uneducated mite and I was indignant.

Poor little mite my arse, I told her, get a mirror, put your hand down there.

Take a look while you're taking a piss.

What's wrong with you girls?

And what did you do with your entire childhood?

At this stage I began to accuse her of telling me fairytales.

No child doesn't take a good look and feel around, and no adult doesn't refresh that knowledge on a weekly basis.

She laughed again, and so did I.

So.

The session was an unlikely success, I'll tell you.

I felt much better afterwards.

She promised to go shopping before our next session and so did I.

She told me I was the most honest client she had ever had and I told her she was doing a really good job.

I thought I might stick around to help her out.

Shore up her self-esteem.

That sort of thing.

Honestly, there is so much work to do in this town, style-wise, you could devote a lifetime to it.

So much raw need.

It's just sheer charity to give back a little of what I know.

SCENE EIGHTEEN

THERESE *is with* LIAM *when* MIKE *enters.*

MIKE: Hi.
LIAM: Hi.
MIKE: Hi, Therese.
THERESE: Hi, Mike.

> MIKE *sits down. He stares at them.*

MIKE: You've found him.
THERESE: No.
MIKE: Maybe.
THERESE: No.
MIKE: [*to* LIAM] Why is she here then?
THERESE: I just came to see how you were doing.

> MIKE *looks at* THERESE *and* LIAM.

MIKE: Tell me.
LIAM: Mike.
MIKE: You're both terrible liars.

> LIAM *looks at* THERESE.

LIAM: A possibility has emerged.
MIKE: So go there. Take me there. I'll identify him.
LIAM: There's no location.

> *Pause.*

THERESE: It's just a listing. On Grindr.
MIKE: And is it him?
THERESE: There's no photo. It may not be him.
MIKE: You think it could be.

LIAM: But she can't accuse someone randomly.

Pause. MIKE *looks at them both.*

MIKE: No.

LIAM: What?

MIKE: You're not doing it.

LIAM: Why?

MIKE: I love you. And I won't let you meet with him.

Pause.

LIAM: You love me?

MIKE: Of course I love you.

LIAM: Like I love you?

MIKE: Yes, probably better because I do most things better than you.

THERESE: I'll let you two discuss it.

LIAM: You say this in front of a stranger.

MIKE: You wanted dinner and a candle?

LIAM: The fuck yes, I wanted dinner and a candle.

MIKE: I thought you knew.

LIAM: I didn't know. You never said.

MIKE: So. I said.

They smile at each other, shyly.

THERESE: Get back to me when you've made a decision. Especially don't arrange a hook-up without telling me where it's going to be.

MIKE: He's not going.

LIAM: Just consider it.

MIKE: Absolutely not.

LIAM: [*to* THERESE] I'll let you know where.

THERESE *exits.*

You're right. Of course I can't meet him.

MIKE: Not on your own.

LIAM: I arrange to meet him somewhere public, just to identify him, and I refuse to go anywhere with him on my own.

MIKE: Yes, that could work.

LIAM: So now you want me to go?

MIKE: Yes, because I want to come.

LIAM *shakes his head.*

If it's him, how will we know where he goes when he leaves you?

LIAM: Therese will follow him.

MIKE: She won't be able to do that. We'll follow him and then I'll beat the shit out of him.

LIAM: Then he'll never be charged.

MIKE: I don't want him to be charged. I want to cripple him like he's crippled me.

    Pause.

LIAM: Yes.

MIKE: Great.

LIAM: Did you mean what you said before?

MIKE: Yes.

    Pause.

LIAM: When you go to get your hair cut, does your hairdresser give you a scalp massage?

MIKE: When she puts on the conditioner.

LIAM: Can I show you?

MIKE: You want to give me a scalp massage?

LIAM: I want to give you a scalp massage.

    LIAM *gives* MIKE *a scalp massage.*

You don't want to be with a friend.

    LIAM *continues with the massage.*

Friends are full of contradictions, we want it but we don't want it. And friends like me live more in our heads than our bodies.

    He is stroking along MIKE*'s body, very lightly, teasingly.* MIKE *is still fully clothed.*

And there's a slow passion to it, more of an aching than a passion.

    He begins to move his hand lightly around MIKE*'s nipples.*

A sleight of hand that can be too sleight of hand if undertaken by someone who doesn't know what they're doing.

    He moves his hand to the inside of MIKE*'s thighs.*

The intimacy of it can unlock you in the most appalling ways.

    He moves MIKE*'s arms above his head.*

So that you shake with longing, so that you vibrate with a need to be tasted and touched and held, close, sweating and breathing hard.

He stands back and does not touch MIKE. MIKE *arches his back as* LIAM *speaks.*

As if your skin were made of soft, warm jelly that, when pressed into another, becomes salty and sweet, and the warm, red jelly of yourself mixes like water with the soft, wet jelly of the other. And you don't know where your skin begins or ends and your bones are like hard, hot limbs of knitting rhythm. And your throat is dry with your rasping breath and your mouth contorts with the pain of the waiting and the trying and the concentrating until you break into a thousand parts, a gel cap broken with liquid messy all over you, and it's terrible and wonderful and shuddering and done.

They stare at each other.

Think hard about whether you want to be with a friend.

LIAM *exits.*

SCENE NINETEEN

LORENA *may be present in this scene.*

MIKE: When I was assaulted, when I was raped, because that really did happen. What I mean is… people talk about wanting justice. I don't want justice. I think Liam wants justice. Whereas I want really nasty, lowbrow revenge. I want brutal… law-into-your-own-hands revenge, yeah. And you ask me what I would like to see in a play about gay men in Broome. I would like to see a full-on vicarious humiliation and assault on someone who is a homosexual rapist. And I would like you to market it to every gay man and every lesbian and every straight person who has ever been bashed or humiliated and promote it as an opportunity to let them sit there and watch someone who symbolises the person who attacked them be really badly bashed, even to death. I want, basically, live revenge porn. That's what I would call a good night in the theatre. And not for cathartic redemption, nah. Just for plain, old, vicarious satisfaction.

Which is why I'm not really interested in theatre at all. Because in theatre as I understand it you have to be basically humanitarian, I mean, when I was in Sydney there was this flush of stuff about paedophiles and it was all about how there are two sides to every story and it's complicated and yeah, the crime was condemned, but there was all this kind of liberal bullshit about how it's complex and nuanced and fucking fuck that shit. If you're someone who has been raped, trust me, you don't want to go and see some middle-class rant about how complicated it is. And here's my call, like it or not those people, those theatre-makers, are basically acting as apologists for rapists.

Hard line? Hard as it goes. 'Cause that's my edges now, you see. I basically want to hold those words down and bash them to death. So, seriously, if you squib this, if you write some twisted, dysfunction version of me, who nevertheless, in the end, learns that hatred only hurts himself, and justice is better than revenge, and is tempted to cut off his attacker's balls but in the end decides to take the high road and forgive him and forgive himself, that will be a betrayal of who I am and what I wanted. 'Cause I would slice that dipshit's nuts off as easily as cutting the top off a tomato. Because I want ugly, ugly, ugly pain for this man who dared, who *dared* to think he could take something from me that I wasn't willing to give. Yeah.

Stick that in your play and smoke it.

SCENE TWENTY

RODNEY *enters.*

RODNEY: You feeling better?

MIKE: Yeah, thanks, Rodney.

RODNEY: It's just Liam mentioned that you were struggling…

MIKE: I don't really want to talk about it, Rodney, if you don't mind.

RODNEY: Not to me.

MIKE: I don't want to be rude.

RODNEY: No, I only meant you seem to be enjoying talking about things with that Lorena, so I thought it helped, you know, getting it off your chest.

MIKE: Well, it does.

    Pause.

RODNEY: Unusual to be able to talk about it. To find the words. Sometimes putting it into words can make it too real.

MIKE: She has a knack.

RODNEY: She came looking for it.

MIKE: You think?

RODNEY: I think she finds this story wherever she goes.

MIKE: Maybe because this story is wherever she goes.

RODNEY: Makes you wonder about her story though, doesn't it?

Pause.

MIKE: Not really. I hadn't given it any thought.

RODNEY: Well, that's the pleasure of being interviewed, isn't it? Not having to reciprocate, you know… listening.

MIKE: I guess so.

RODNEY: Have you noticed, when an interviewer starts to tell you their story, how it's kind of annoying…

MIKE: [*laughing*] 'I thought this was about me.'

RODNEY: It's terrible but you're not the least bit interested in their story. Not at all.

MIKE: Sometimes you might be.

RODNEY: [*thinking*] Nah. Doubt it.

They laugh.

But I mean that's the job, you didn't ask to be interested in them and you only would be if she was, I dunno, susceptible, for some reason.

MIKE: To what?

RODNEY: I dunno.

MIKE: How do you mean, susceptible?

RODNEY: Maybe I mean suggestible.

MIKE: You mean like, open?

RODNEY: Yeah, empathetic to a certain kind of story.

MIKE: Well, that's different to suggestible.

RODNEY: Yeah, but that would make her story significant, then you would need to hear it.

MIKE: What are you talking about, Rodney?

RODNEY: I'm talking about doing whatever it takes to get it out, recover, and be able to move on to another relationship. Especially with someone as incredible as Liam. Whatever you have to do, do it. If I could go back. If I could go back to when I really needed another person before I became so… If I could go back and try to forge that link instead of just resigning myself to never having that. I would. In a heartbeat.

MIKE *nods.*

SCENE TWENTY-ONE

LORENA: When I was fourteen I had a crush on a boy and so I did what any southern suburbs Australian teenage girl does when she finds herself in the daze of such a feeling. I bought myself a new bikini from Target. It was yellow with orange spots and it looked, well, it looked terrific. We had agreed to meet at the Caars Park public pool. Let's call this boy Ratko because he was Yugoslavian. Me and Ratko were going to meet him and his friends at Caars Park and have a swim. What could be better? I didn't have any friends with me, I knew this boy because he was the older cousin of one of our neighbours, one of my younger brother's friends. I arranged to meet him at the pool, a public place. Why should I have any friends with me? I didn't have that many friends anyway. I mean, I had friends, but mostly I hung out on weeknights and weekends with a gang from my street—I played cricket and listened to music in other people's front rooms—my house being a kind of alcoholic parent no-go zone. So I had friends but not ones that I went places with. Like pools.

> *As she speaks,* LORENA *removes her dress, underneath is a bikini in exactly the colours she describes.*

So I get the bus to Caars Park pool and I meet Ratko poolside. He knows I'm keen and I'm loving his attention. The full force of his undivided attention. You know the way teenage girls are with boys who like them. Dazzled. So we dive in, swim around a bit, and in the water he comes on to me pretty quickly. Grabs me and holds me to him and kisses me and the feel of our near naked bodies pressed against each other in the water was pretty nice actually. I felt that he was hard and underwater he was holding my bum cheeks and pulling me toward him, rubbing me slightly on his wet costume. I was giggling and squealing a little but he had a firm grip on me and I wasn't really trying to get away. He was still holding me pressed hard against him when he suddenly reached under the midsection of my bikini and stuck his fingers up my vagina. At first I was so shocked I just froze. Then I struggled to get away but he was much stronger than me. We were floating around in the deep end of the pool, in what looked like a romantic embrace, but was actually a young man with his fingers up me. And every time I struggled he would jam his fingers harder into me.

It was a surreal feeling to be in a public place, a public pool, with children and adults and others splashing all around me, and me, locked in an embrace with a boy who was violating me with his fingers. I was in such a state of disbelief that I just kept floating around with him, still locked in this submerged assault, and every time I told him to let go or tried to push him away he pushed more fingers into me and pushed them deeper and harder. It was a brutal lesson in the ineffectiveness of my voice and the powerlessness of my body. There was also no disputing that Ratko had gone from the amorous love interest to a nasty prick who was having fun holding me hostage in front of his mates. His touch was not designed to arouse me but only to subject me to his will. After what felt like hours of this, but may have been about fifteen to twenty minutes, another of his friends came splashing over and he too was smiling. That's when Ratko pulled his fingers out from inside me but, still holding me from behind, let his friend shove his hands down the front of my bikini. Now I screamed and struggled harder, but in the chaos and mayhem and boisterous good fun of a public pool no-one thought my screams were anything more than high jinks. Ratko's friend now proceeded to digitally assault me underwater where no-one could see. In broad daylight, in a public pool, he rubbed his hard penis on my thigh and jammed his fingers into my vagina. I was kind of sandwiched between the two boys and they were jumping up and down on the bottom of the pool, as if we were in a kind of crazy swimming game.

Ratko let four of his friends have a turn with me between them. No-one in the pool noticed, no-one on the sides noticed. No-one did anything at all. Mostly I was mute with shock, but eventually I started crying and blubbering to be let go. When snot started running down my face and I couldn't wipe it away because of my pinned-back arms, Ratko let me go. He and his mates climbed out of the pool and I stayed in the water, pressed against the side of the cold tiles till I saw them grab their towels and retreat to the change room. I looked around, sure that someone, anyone, someone must have noticed what had happened but nup, nothing. Not a suspicious side-ways glance from even the geekiest of kids. I clearly remember that my ears seemed to be, um, not blocked, but the sound of the world was turned down, as if it was all now behind some kind of screen.

I got out of the pool and found my towel and sat on the side in the sun, shivering. I didn't tell anyone, I didn't scream, I didn't even really have a name for what had happened to me except that I knew I didn't like it. I had gone to the pool with Ratko in my new bikini and I had liked it when he first slid up on me. So in my mind I guess I had brought it on. But I never even thought about it like that. I went to the change rooms, took off my wet bikini and when I got home I threw it in the bin. My mother asked me why I was throwing it away and I told her it was because another girl at school had bought one the same colour and I didn't want to be the same.

I have written about some pretty horrific sexual assaults and the first thing I learnt was that victims should not compare themselves to other victims, you know, ranking the assault to determine if it's re-ally *worth* being ashamed of. If I put my experience beside that of the woman who explained to me how her schizophrenic father hooked her up to the lawnmower and used the electrical current to electrocute her genitals then my experience is going to pale in comparison.

I have carried with me, since childhood, the shame, the confusion, the fear of someone finding out, the feeling of being dirty, the sense of being invisible, the perversion of desire, the burden of being victimised. But the same experiences which have crippled me with doubt and low self-esteem have also given me empathy and understanding and compassion which are rare and cherished gifts. The ability to listen and believe.

SCENE TWENTY-TWO

LIAM & MIKE: [*sung*] The gays in Broome they travel south,
      They visit family do's,
      But three days into holidays
      They'd rather be in Broome.
      They like the inclusivity
      Where labels go away,
      They'll paint the town in rainbow pride

And never hide away.

LIAM: Hi, John. I'm Liam.

JOHN: Hi, Liam.

LIAM: Where are you from?

JOHN: Let's just get on with it, shall we?

LIAM: Don't be like that.

JOHN: Like what, Liam?

LIAM: Cagey. Anyone would think you had something to hide.

JOHN: Do I turn you on or not, Liam? That's all you need to know.

LIAM: Turn me on?

JOHN: Yeah?

LIAM: How would I know?

JOHN: There are ways of telling.

> JOHN *reaches for* LIAM's *crotch.* LIAM *is flaccid.* JOHN *pulls his hand away.*

LIAM: Actually, you don't particularly.

JOHN: What?

LIAM: That's because self-hating, closeted rapists don't, usually.

> JOHN *pulls back.*

JOHN: What is this?

> MIKE *emerges.*

MIKE: I don't think we gave it a name, did we, Liam?

LIAM: No, but I guess we could call it payday.

MIKE: Payback day.

JOHN: You.

LIAM: Isn't that sweet, he remembered your name.

JOHN: I don't know what you think you're playing at here.

MIKE: I don't think we're playing at all, are we, Liam?

LIAM: Not playing as in pretending, no.

JOHN: This is bullshit.

MIKE: This is paying back how you raped me, bashed me, and left me to die, you piece of shit.

LIAM: And so today we're going to give you a taste of what that is like.

> *They grab* JOHN, *between them they hold him down, facedown on the bed. He struggles but they have a good grip. They put some-*

thing over his mouth so that he cannot scream, then they pull down his trousers so that his arse is exposed.

There is a knock at the door.

They look at each other. There is another knock.

Who is it?

THERESE: It's me. Therese.

LIAM: Go away, Therese.

THERESE: I can't do that, Liam, let me in.

Pause.

Let me in right now.

MIKE *moves onto the prostrate man, shoving his head into the bed.*

LIAM *gets up and goes to the door. He opens it and* THERESE *walks in.*

Get off him, Mike.

MIKE: It's not what you think this is.

THERESE: What do I think this is?

MIKE: You think this is the guy who attacked me. But it's not.

THERESE: No?

MIKE: No. Liam, take off his gag.

LIAM *takes off his gag.*

John, this is Detective Constable Skyler. And this is a consenting threesome between adults, isn't it?

After a moment, JOHN *nods.*

THERESE: I can see the likeness.

MIKE: Gay men, it's a look.

THERESE: A consenting threesome?

LIAM: That's right.

MIKE: Police got no place in the bedroom of three consenting adults.

THERESE: That's not what this is.

LIAM: Yeah.

Pause.

JOHN: Hey, this was fun, but I gotta go now, guys.

JOHN *begins to leave.*

THERESE: How are you travelling, John?

JOHN: Driving.

THERESE: Okay then. Licence.

JOHN: What?

THERESE: I would like to ensure that you have a driver's licence.

> JOHN *takes his pack off his back and reaches inside. Instead of pulling out a wallet with his licence, he pulls out a knife.*

> THERESE *is next to the door.*

JOHN: Get out of my way.

THERESE: You're not really pulling a knife, sir.

JOHN: I just want to leave.

THERESE: Put down the knife, sir.

JOHN: I said get out of my way, bitch, right now.

> MIKE *walks over to the door.*

MIKE: You're not going anywhere, trash.

JOHN: Get out of my way, both of you, or I'll run you through.

MIKE: Bring it on.

JOHN: I will.

MIKE: Oh, I'm the last person you have to convince of that.

JOHN: I'll cut you up like a stupid, fat cow.

MIKE: Run me through, Starman, run me through now.

LIAM: Mike, what are you doing?

> MIKE *does not answer but runs at* JOHN, *the knife going into his chest.*

MIKE: Ho, that hurts.

LIAM: Mike.

THERESE: Don't take it out.

> *She rushes at* JOHN *and struggles with him to the ground.*

Call the ambulance.

LIAM: My phone is out of battery.

THERESE: See if he has one.

JOHN: Get off me.

> LIAM *finds* JOHN*'s phone.*

LIAM: I'm calling the ambulance. Right now. Blackberry. Um. Phone,

phone I'm hitting the app for phone. Phone, now what? Options, options, go into keypad and dial triple-oh. Someone will answer.

Pause.

Police, fire or ambulance. Ambulance please. My friend has been stabbed. Address. We are in Broome. We are at the Blue Boab Motor Inn. Yes, he is conscious. No, don't remove the knife.

JOHN: This is bullshit.

MIKE: Your fingerprints are on the knife.

JOHN: You ran at me.

MIKE: Yeah, to stop you from stabbing the police officer who you were threatening. You can't wriggle out of this one, trash. You're going in there with all those murderers and drug takers and they are going to shove it up your arse so far that you're going to be gagging on your porridge.

JOHN: This is bullshit.

THERESE: Mike, I advise you stay calm, try not to speak.

JOHN: I didn't stab him, he ran at me. You saw it.

THERESE: Did I?

JOHN: This is bullshit.

THERESE: I saw a brave man defending a police officer.

JOHN: And you can't talk to me without reading me my rights.

THERESE: You mean, 'You have the right to remain silent'.

JOHN: Yeah, all that.

THERESE: We don't have Miranda rights in Australia.

JOHN: What?

THERESE: You've watched too much television, sir.

JOHN: This is unbelievable.

THERESE: What's your name?

JOHN: I have the right to remain silent, you bitch.

THERESE: Actually, you do have the right to remain silent under common law. But I don't have to advise you of that, so what's your name?

JOHN: This is bullshit.

THERESE: Liam, can you check the backpack? Carefully, we don't know what else is in there.

LIAM: I don't want to leave Mike.

THERESE: Mike is all good as long as you don't remove the knife.

LIAM *goes to the backpack and removes the wallet.*

LIAM: John Fandrich.

THERESE: F.A.N.D.R.I.C.H?

JOHN: This is total bullshit.

THERESE: You'll be charged with grievous bodily harm and with sexual assault, Mr Fandrich. This is your attacker, Mike?

MIKE *nods.*

MIKE: How long will he get for that?

JOHN: Nothing, because I didn't do it.

MIKE: Shut it, trash.

THERESE: Six years for the bodily harm, up to twenty for the sexual assault, depending on the judge.

JOHN: Which you'll never prove.

MIKE *takes the knife out of his own chest.*

MIKE: And for murder?

LIAM: Don't leave me!

JOHN: This is such bullshit.

THERESE: Liam, try to keep pressure on the wound. Mike, what are you doing?

MIKE: But he will, won't he? He'll get more for murder?

JOHN: This is such unadulterated bullshit. You are crazy, man. I'm not wearing this.

THERESE *gets off* JOHN *to go to* MIKE.

But MIKE *runs over to* JOHN *and holds him from behind.*

MIKE: You have the right to remain silent, Starman.

He slices JOHN*'s jugular. Blood goes everywhere.* JOHN *dies a gurgling death.*

MIKE *collapses, giggling quietly.*

THERESE: Shit.

LIAM: Shit.

MIKE: Aaagh.

THERESE: Keep pressure on the wound.

SCENE TWENTY-THREE

LORENA: Do you think I might be able to speak to Therese?

LIAM: No, she's been transferred.

LORENA: Well, I'm sure it's to somewhere with a mobile phone.

LIAM: Still.

LORENA: No?

LIAM: You're not really going to put it in your play, are you? The whole story, like the murder and that?

LORENA: Well… yeah. I am.

LIAM: Nah, I don't think that's a good idea.

LORENA: Right.

LIAM: It's not something you want out there… you know. Made public.

LORENA: Okay. But I've got to ask. Why did you tell me if you didn't want it out there?

LIAM: Yeah.

LORENA: I mean, you have signed a release and everything, saying I can include it.

LIAM: Right. Yeah. But the thing is…

Pause.

We may have exaggerated a little bit.

LORENA: What do you mean exaggerated?

LIAM: I just want this to stop now, Lorena.

LORENA: Okay.

LIAM: The thing with Mike is attention. You see, and I understand that. He dresses up and it provokes people and he likes that. And I like that.

LORENA: I love that about Mike.

LIAM: No matter how I do this you're going to hate us.

LORENA: Of course I won't.

LIAM: But you will you will you will.

LORENA: Liam, it's okay.

LIAM: No, it has to stop now. It's gone too far. I understood when it was… like… there's things he can't say and then… he was really losing it… I just wanted to bring him back from the edge and… you did… you did… this did.

LORENA: Please don't get upset.

LIAM: Because you asked. You asked him what happened. And in his mind what happened has been... changed.

LORENA: Changed how?

LIAM: He never reported it, Lorena. And so it's grown into this fantasy, this hate-filled thing.

LORENA: But he did report it.

LIAM: No.

LORENA: I don't understand.

LIAM: I'm sorry. It started off as kind of exaggerated and then it just took on a life of its own.

LORENA: What do you mean exaggerated?

LIAM: I mean lied.

LORENA: Lied?

LIAM: A bit.

LORENA: Which bit?

LIAM: All of it.

LORENA: All of what happened to Mike?

LIAM: Sort of.

> *Pause.* LORENA *involuntarily moves backward away from him, like a crab.*

LORENA: No.

LIAM: Sorry.

LORENA: No.

LIAM: Yeah.

LORENA: You can't have.

LIAM: I know.

LORENA: You lied?

LIAM: We told you the version of John that Mike has sort of dressed up.

> *Pause.*

LORENA: No, you didn't.

LIAM: Yeah.

LORENA: No, this is your way of getting me not to put it in, right?

LIAM: No, Lorena, he made it up and I went along with it.

LORENA: I don't believe you.

LIAM: You should believe me.

LORENA: Please tell me you didn't lie.

MIKE *enters.*

MIKE: You told her?

LIAM: Yep.

MIKE: I can tell. From her face. She's not pleased.

LIAM: She doesn't believe me.

LORENA: I don't believe you.

MIKE: You know that's exactly what we thought you'd say so many times during the interview.

LIAM: As the story got bigger and bigger.

MIKE: Blood. Stabbings. Police corruption.

LIAM: All with lurid detail.

LORENA: You were never raped?

> *Pause.*

MIKE: I was raped just like that, by a person, my partner, who I'd been with for nearly a year. All I've changed is the setting. He'd been controlling and then he became violent and I was so ashamed I couldn't tell anyone. And then he raped me.

> *Pause.*

And I left him and then I came to Broome.

LORENA: Why didn't you tell me that?

MIKE: It's not much of a story.

LORENA: It's an horrific story.

MIKE: Not really. Not like bashed in a dress at the Broome races and then a knife to the throat in a motel clinch.

> *Pause.*

LORENA: [*angry*] And that's why you lied? Because it's a better story?

MIKE: Well, you're the student of human nature. You tell me.

LORENA: No-one has ever lied to me before.

LIAM: Yeah, they have.

MIKE: Why do you tell other people's stories?

LORENA: What?

MIKE: Why have you always told other people's stories and not your own?

LORENA: I've told my own story through other people.

MIKE: And that's what I've done too.

LORENA: Not like this. Not a complete fabrication.

MIKE: And is that what this is?

LORENA: [*furious*] Well, I'm asking what this is?

MIKE: This is what I live with.

LORENA: What?

MIKE: John may not be real, but he is true.

LORENA: In your mind.

LIAM: Don't say it like it's nothing.

LORENA: What?

MIKE: Listen. I tell you what actually happened to me and I flip it off because that's what I need to do. Pfff. It was nothing. But just because I tell myself it's nothing and I tell other people it's nothing… doesn't mean there's nothing in here.

LORENA: Yeah, well, I don't deal with in there. I deal with what really happened.

LIAM: Why? You're not a journalist, are you?

LORENA: No, I'm not, but I'm after veracity, I'm after authenticity.

MIKE: Listen, sweetness, you want to know why? Because this is my life in here. In here, John stalks me and controls me and assaults me, over and over and over. And the only way I can make it real, the only way I can dodge all my own… stuff… about how this should have been the love of my life… how he was the one and then he was this… monster, is to make him into this… I thought you might understand.

Pause.

LORENA: You should report it.

MIKE: Yeah. Probably.

LIAM: When you're ready.

Pause.

MIKE: The part about coming to Broome and falling for your best friend, that is all…

LIAM: True.

MIKE *and* LIAM *kiss.*

MIKE: And you.

LORENA: What?

MIKE: Have lied.

LORENA: No.

LIAM: Yes.

LORENA: No.

MIKE: You have.

LIAM: You've shaped the story, though.

Pause.

LORENA: Yes.

MIKE: Which is fine.

LIAM: Because your job is fascination.

MIKE: You are a fascinator.

Pause.

LORENA: You're a pair of lying, poofter bastards.

MIKE: We deserve that

LORENA: Cocksucking liars.

LIAM: So can John be real?

LORENA: No?

MIKE: He is.

LORENA: Is he?

LIAM: You can make him real.

LORENA: Yes. No.

Long pause.

Maybe.

They exit. LORENA *sits listening to her recording device. Rodney may be present elsewhere on stage or as a voice recording.*

RODNEY: I do know some guys who have never come to grips with their sexuality. And… one of them is in air-conditioning, in Perth though, and he's never told his mates or his clients that he's gay… and he gets invited out with a partner and he says to me, 'What do I do?', and I say, 'Tell 'em you're gay and they'll still accept you and the ones who don't, piss them off'. He's still gripped by fear.

He's in his sixties now and he's going to die, living a lie. And he says to me, 'It's private, that stuff is my private self'. Different generation. But you still get that in this generation too. You'd be surprised. People who can't say things about themselves, so they tell stories. Maybe they're not lying, they're telling the truth their way. I think people can handle anything about anyone except a lie. I dunno. There's a lot of people in the Kimberley and in the Territory with a lot of secrets. Hell, there's a lot of people everywhere with secrets. You must get to hear a lot of them, I guess. I'll tell you mine. Before I came to Broome I was living a version of something. Now I'm going to be me. Any version of me that suits me. Okay?

LORENA *sits, contemplating. Lights fade.*

THE END

GRIFFIN THEATRE COMPANY PRESENTS
THE WORLD PREMIERE OF

LADIES DAY
BY ALANA VALENTINE
DIRECTED BY DARREN YAP
5 FEBRUARY - 26 MARCH

Director Darren Yap

Set & Costume Designer James Browne

Sound Designer & Composer Max Lambert

Lighting Designer Hugh Hamilton

Stage Manager Cara Woods

With Matthew Backer, Wade Briggs, Lucia Mastrantone and Elan Zavelsky

SBW STABLES THEATRE
5 FEBRUARY - 26 MARCH

GTC
RHO
IEM
FAP
FTA
IRN
NEY

GRIFFIN THEATRE COMPANY

Presented in association with

SYDNEY GAY AND LESBIAN MARDI GRAS

Government Partners

Australian Government

Australia Council for the Arts

NSW GOVERNMENT | Arts NSW

The research and writing of *Ladies Day* was supported by the Literature Fund of the Australia Council for the Arts.

PLAYWRIGHT'S NOTE

Ladies Day has benefitted from the generous self-disclosure of men who identify as homosexual living in Broome, elsewhere in the Kimberley and also in the Northern Territory, especially Darwin and Katherine. Given my own sustained relationship with the GLBTI communities of Sydney (and elsewhere) it would be fair to say that much of my life has contributed to the portraits of the characters in this drama. The line between truth and fiction is one which audiences themselves must draw. My sincere contract with the audience for *Ladies Day* is that I hope this work is no less true for being an artifice of conflations, amalgamations and combinations of stories drawn from real life.

I acknowledge that the custodians of the land around Broome are the Yawuru people and I pay my respects to their elders past and present. I thank the two elders of that community who made me welcome there during my visit. I also acknowledge the Dharug and Cadigal people of the land of the Sydney basin on which this work will first play. My thanks to Adam Sasinowski, Chris West, Damian Pio, Terry Hurrey, Thomas McKenzie, Max Middleton, Lorrae Coffin, Toni Tapp-Coutts, Sharne McGee, Vicki Gordon for research assistance, and several others who wish to remain anonymous.

The research and writing of *Ladies Day* was supported by the Literature Board of the Australia Council for the Arts, and I acknowledge Lee Lewis as a visionary artistic partner.

Alana Valentine
Writer

DIRECTOR'S NOTE

Ladies Day is an important, honest and confronting play. It's not only an intelligent piece about people living on the margins who often don't get a chance to tell their stories, but it also hits you in the gut.

For me the stories of men not being able to 'come out' as gay because of their upbringing or culture - or older men who will die never 'coming out' to their friends as 'homosexual', (it will be their secret) saddens me because it has been my journey too. Also, it's a great night in the theatre!

Alana has taken her interviews and crafted them into an intricate, entertaining story. And as some of these characters are based on real interviews it make us responsible to honour these characters which is a great motivation. The stories swing from being candid, to outrageous and then raw. For instance Mike speaks about love and violence and vengeance. We watch him hide from his pain and we want sweet justice for him. We want him to find comfort from his pain. And so this is what the play is good at doing. We invest so much into these characters because the play digs deep into areas when the truth can be too brutal and too ugly to deal with.

Any new work is an honour and a challenge. You want to find the perfect communion between the story and the audience. The perfect balance between the intellect and the soul where we ultimately will feel something deeply. And this would not have been possible without Alana's beautiful script and insight into humanity.

Thank you to the Griffin for developing *Ladies Day*, the creative team and our actors who brought the play to life.

Darren Yap
Director

Alana Valentine

Playwright

Ladies Day is Alana Valentine's Griffin debut. Her theatre credits in Sydney include *Parramatta Girls* and *Run Rabbit Run* for Belvoir; *Head Full of Love* for Queensland Theatre Company and Darwin Festival, which raised over $60,000 in audience donations for the Purple House kidney dialysis unit in Alice Springs. Upcoming works include: *Cold Light* for The Street Theatre Canberra; *One Billion Beats* (co-written and co-directed with Romaine Moreton) for Campbelltown Arts Centre; *The Tree Widows* for Tasmanian Theatre Company which she will also direct; *Letters to Lindy* for Merrigong Theatre Company followed by Canberra Theatre Centre and Seymour Centre; and *SOFT REVOLUTION: Shafana and Aunt Sarrinah* at the Venus Theatre in Maryland, USA.

In 2014 Alana won the BBC International Radio Competition and an AWGIE Award for Community/ Youth Theatre for *Comin' Home Soon*; in 2013 she won three AWGIE Awards including the Major Award and the inaugural David Williamson Award for Excellence in Writing for the Australian Theatre for *Grounded*; and in 2012 she won the S.T.A.G.E International Award for *Ear to the Edge of Time*. Alana's plays are published by Currency Press and her website is www.alanavalentine.com

Darren Yap
Director

Darren recently was the Artistic Festival Consultant for the Opening of the National Gallery of Singapore's celebrations. He directed *Miracle City* for Luckiest Productions at the Hayes Theatre, *The Serpent's Table* with Lee Lewis for Griffin's 2014 season presented by Performance 4a and the Sydney Festival at CarriageWorks and *A Murder is Announced* for Louise Withers and Associates. Other directing credits include the world premiere of *Man of Letters* for the Singapore Repertory Theatre and *The Admiral's Odyssey* for Action Theatre, Singapore. Darren's large scale events include the City of Sydney's Chinese New Year Parade for two years, *SpongeBob Parade Pants* for Nickelodeon and Segment Director of the *Closing Ceremony of the 15th Asian Games* in Qatar.

He was Associate Director of *King Kong* for Global Creatures, Miss Saigon for Cameron Mackintosh (West End, Tokyo, Korea, Holland and Australia) and *Mamma Mia* (10th Anniversary Australian tour). He will be directing Alana Valentine's *Letters to Lindy*, based on the Lindy Chamberlain story, at Merrigong in 2016 and a new musical, *The Great Wall* based on a Chinese Folk tale about Meng Jiang Yu and the First Emperor of China.

James Browne
Set & Costume Designer

James has previously worked with Griffin Theatre Company as Set and Costume Designer on *Beached*. His other theatre credits include, for the Australian Institute of Music: *Sweeny Todd* (Concert Venue); for Darlinghurst Theatre Company: *Ordinary Days*; for Hayes Theatre: *Dogfight*; for Monkey Baa Theatre Company: *Pete the Sheep*; for Regal Theatre: *Certified Male*; for Seymour Centre: *Fat Swan*; for the Sydney Opera House: *Just for Laughs*; for Theatre Royal: *Side by Side*; and Reg Livermore's *Turns*.

James' recent set work includes *The Very Hungry Caterpillar* and both set and costume for *Velvet*. Previous costume design work includes, for Opera Australia: Graeme Murphy's *Aida* (Associate Designer); Sydney Dance Company's *New Breed*; and Stuart Maunder's *Shout!* Previous event design work includes: *Love Cooking Festival* (London); Jamie Oliver's live stadium show; Netball World Cup opening ceremony; and Pacha Sydney.

Max Lambert
Composer & Sound Designer

Max is one of Australia's most talented composers, arrangers, musicians and musical directors. Composing credits include work for Sydney, Melbourne and Queensland Theatre Companies, Sydney Dance Company and The Australian Ballet. Recording album credits include: Kate Ceberano, Wendy Matthews, Grace Knight, Vince Jones, Renee Geyer, Paul Kelly, Iva Davies and Icehouse. Max's film credits include: George Miller's *Happy Feet*; Gillian Armstrong's *The Last Days of Chez Nous*. His Musical theatre credits include, David Atkins' *Hot Shoe Shuffle*.

Max's Musical Directorship credits include Opening and Closing Ceremonies of *Sydney 2000 Olympic Games*; *2002 Commonwealth Games* (Manchester); *2006 Asian Games* (Doha, Qatar). His Musical Supervisor credits include: ARIA award-winning production *The Boy From Oz*, *Hairspray*, *Fame*, *King Kong* and *Strictly Ballroom the Musical*. The revival of Max's musical *Miracle City* (co-written with Nick Enright) was a runaway success at The Hayes Theatre in 2014.

Roger Lock
Associate Composer & Sound Designer

Guitarist, producer and composer Roger Lock grew up on the Mid-North Coast of New South Wales, Australia and after graduating from Sydney's Conservatorium High School, moved to England to study classical guitar. From 2000 - 2006 he attended the Mozarteum University of Salzburg studying guitar, composition and music technology. During this period he played concerts in Austria, Germany, Italy, Sweden, Spain, Hungary and Taiwan. In 2007 Roger moved to Vienna and greatly diversified his musical activities. As a session musician he was very active as a concert and recording artist, producing several albums with Yorgos Nousis, Laetitia Ribeiro, Dr. Opin and Troebinger.

Since returning to Australia in 2009 Roger has worked as a freelance producer, composer and instrumentalist with the Eminence Symphony Orchestra. He has also worked with Emma Sholl, Jane Rosenson, TaikOz and his band project Roger Vs. The Man. He has taught at AICM, AIM, UNSW and the Sydney Conservatorium of Music and currently runs the Cranbrook High Recording Studio.

Hugh Hamilton

Lighting Designer

This is Hugh's first show for Griffin. His theatre credits in design include, for Luckiest Productions: *Miracle City*; for Sydney Dance Company: *Freefall*; for Sydney Theatre Company: *Del Del*; for Legs On the Wall: *Eora*, *Crossing* and *On the Case*; for Bel Rosa Opera Company: *HMS Pinafore*; for Orial: *I Am My Own Wife*; for Opera Hunter: *Madama Butterfly* and for Brink Productions: *Ursula*.

He has also been Associate Lighting Designer on *Wicked* (Korean Language), *The King and I*, *The Addams Family Musical*, *Jersey Boys*, *Legally Blonde*, *Rock of Ages*, *Guys and Dolls*, and *Tivoli*. He has worked extensively in Asia as the Assistant Lighting Designer and Programmer on *Miss Saigon*, *Mamma Mia 10th Anniversary Tour*, *Phantom of the Opera* and *CATS*, as well as Production Electrician on *Wicked*, Lighting Programmer on *Les Misérables*, and original Lighting Programmer on *Priscilla: Queen of the Desert the Musical* and *Love Never Dies*.

Cara Woods

Stage Manager

Cara has been Stage Manager for 2015 Griffin Independent shows: *Five Properties of Chainmale*, *The Dapto Chaser* and *A Riff on Keef: The Human Myth*. *Ladies Day* is Cara's first Main Season show for Griffin. Since graduating from The Actors College of Theatre and Television where she studied an Advanced Diploma of Stage Management, Cara has worked on various independent theatre shows as Stage Manager throughout Sydney. She has also branched out from the independent scene, as a swing on *Strictly Ballroom the Musical* and Stage Manager on *Short + Sweet Voices*.

Elan Zavelsky
Rodney / John / Chorus 2

After returning from a year spent living and traveling in Europe and the Middle East, leading him to focus on a career in the world of mental health, Elan received an out of the blue voicemail from Lee Lewis (who directed him in Bell Shakespeare's 2010 production of *Twelfth Night*) to partake in a new production, *Ladies Day*. Five years after his last onstage performance, he met with Darren and Mel and, to his great delight, joined the *Ladies Day* team. As a gay man himself, he felt it was an important story to tell and is proud to be a part of a production that focuses on a world in which few dare to delve. This is Elan's third production on the SBW Stables stage, having performed in Cry Havoc's *Orestes 2.0* in 2010; and *Arabian Night*, directed by Eamon Flack in 2008. Some of Elan's film and TV credits include: *Crownies*, *Underbelly*, *All Saints* and *The Diplomat*.

Lucia Mastrantone
Lorena / Therese / Chorus 1

Lucia has enjoyed a successful career in theatre, physical theatre, film, television and as a voice artist, with an extensive list of credits. Her theatre credits for the major companies include: for Company B, Belvoir: *The Book of Everything*, *Scorched*, *Macbeth*, *Vicious Angel*, *The Popular Mechanicals 1 & 2*, *Love and Magic in Mamma's Kitchen*; for Bell Shakespeare: *The Duchess of Malfi*; for the State Theatre Company of South Australia: *The Merchant of Venice*, *Six Characters in Search of an Author*, *A Little Drowning*; for Sydney Theatre Company: *Mariage Blanc* and *Romeo and Juliet*; and for Melbourne Theatre Company: *The Venetian Twins*. Lucia's screen appearances include acclaimed TC series' John Edward's *Tangle*, ABC TV's *Rake* and AFI Award-winning film *Look Both Ways*. Lucia is currently co-starring in a new animation comedy series produced by Working Dog called *Pacific Heat*.

Wade Briggs

Mike

Wade graduated from WAAPA in 2010. His theatre credits for Griffin include: *Rust and Bone*; for Crow Crow Theatre Profuctions and Rock Surfers Theatre Company: *K.I.J.E* (directed by Sarah Giles); for Rock Surfers Theatre Company: *Blood Pressure*; for Black Swan State Theatre Company: *The Damned* and most recently *King Lear* for Sydney Theatre Company, directed by Neil Armfield.

Wade's film credits include *What if it Works?*, *The Spirit of the Game* and the short *Yardbird* which won Best Australian Short Film at Sydney Film Festival 2013 and was the only Australian film in competition at the 2012 Cannes Film Festival. Television credits include *Home & Away*, and the ABC/Pivot comedy series *Please Like Me*, written by and starring Josh Thomas.

Matthew Backer

Liam

Matthew is a graduate of the National Institute of Dramatic Art (NIDA). He has previously performed in Griffin's *24 Hour Play Project* and *Uncanny Valley*. His other theatre credits include: for Sydney Theatre Company: *Machinal* and *Orlando*; for Bell Shakespeare: *Henry V* and *The Tempest* (Sydney Theatre Award nomination); for Belvoir: *Kill the Messenger*; for Queensland Theatre Company: *Brisbane*; for Peach Theatre Company: *The History Boys*; for HotHouse Theatre: *Frenzy for Two*; for TheatreWorks: *Private View*; for The Leapfrog Touring Company: *The Chaos Fairy and the Wizard*; for Parade Theatre: *Mr Chicken Goes to Paris*; and for NIDA: *Fortune and Men's Eyes* and *Not I*. His musical theatre credits include, for Dodger Theatricals/New Theatricals/Dainty Consolidated Entertainment/Michael Watt: *Jersey Boys*; and for NIDA: *Assassins* and *I Love You, You're Perfect, Now Change*. His short film credits include *Whispers Among Wolves* (Flickerfest, Sydney Film Festival, Palm Springs Film Festival, Hollywood Film Festival), *Milk & Honey*, *Chicom* and *Oiling Point*. His television credits include *History Hunters* and *Deadly Women*. Matthew was a founding member of the sketch-comedy collective *I'm With Stupid*, which has appeared on ABC iView and ABC2. Matthew was a 2014 recipient of both a Mike Walsh Fellowship and a Gloria Payten and Gloria Dawn Foundations Fellowship, with which he studied improvisational comedy at Upright Citizen's Brigade and People's Improv Theatre in New York City and The Second City in Los Angeles.

ABOUT GRIFFIN THEATRE COMPANY

Griffin Theatre Company is Australia's new writing theatre. For nearly 40 years, Griffin has been dedicated to bringing the best Australian stories to the stage. We have a passion for developing Australian talent, with many of our nation's most celebrated artists starting their professional careers with us.

Griffin is a major force in shaping the future of Australian theatre: it is a home for the courageous and the curious, for the imaginations that inspire us. Iconic Australian stories such as *Lantana*, *The Boys*, *Holding the Man* and *The Heartbreak Kid* had their world premieres at Griffin.

Griffin produces an annual subscription season of four to five Main Season shows by Australian playwrights, and co-presents a season of new work with leading independent artists and special events from producers around the country. We also support artists through professional development opportunities, artist residencies and master classes.

Our home is the historic SBW Stables Theatre, Sydney's most intimate and persuasive space for writers, actors and audiences to meet. We hope to see you here soon.

GRIFFIN THEATRE COMPANY
13 CRAIGEND ST
KINGS CROSS NSW 2011

02 9332 1052
INFO@GRIFFINTHEATRE.COM.AU
GRIFFINTHEATRE.COM.AU

SBW STABLES THEATRE
10 NIMROD ST
KINGS CROSS NSW 2011

BOOKINGS
GRIFFINTHEATRE.COM.AU
02 9361 3817

GTC
RHO
IEM
FAP
FTA
IRN
NEY

STAFF

PRODUCTION DONORS

You made this.

Ladies Day was produced with the support of Griffin Theatre Company's Production Donors. Production Donors make a direct contribution to the costs of staging an individual play, chosen for its unique voice and the strength, insight and candour it brings to the stage.

For further information about the program, please contact our Development Manager on 02 9332 1052.

Production Patrons
Robert Dick
& Erin Shiel
Reay McGuinness
Richard McHugh
& Kate Morgan
Bruce Meagher
& Greg Waters
Richard Weinstein
& Richard Benedict

Production Partners
Cambridge Events
Michael Hobbs
Steve Riethoff
Annabel Ritchie
Diana Simmonds
Jenny & Peter Solomon

GRIFFIN DONORS

Income from Griffin activities covers less than 40% of our operating costs – leaving an ever increasing gap for us to fill through government funding, sponsorship and the generosity of our individual supporters. Your support helps us bridge the gap and keep ticket prices affordable and our work at its best. To make a donation and a difference, contact Griffin on 9332 1052 or donate online at griffintheatre.com.au

Commission $12,500+
Darin Cooper Family
Anthony & Suzanne Maple-Brown

Studio Program
Gil Appleton
James Emmett & Peter Wilson
Limb Family Foundation
Sophie McCarthy
& Antony Green
Rhonda McIver
Geoff & Wendy Simpson
Danielle Smith

Main Stage Donor $5,000 - $10,000
The Sky Foundation
Abraham James

Workshop Donor $1,000-$4,999
Anonymous (5)
Dr Gae Anderson
Ellen Borda
Jane Bridge
Alex Byrne & Sue Hearn
Richard Cottrell
Ros & Paul Espie
John & Libby Fairfax
Jono Gavin
Peter Graves
Larry & Tina Grumley
Judge Joe Harman
James Hartwright & Kerrin D'Arcy
Libby Higgin
Margaret Johnston
Richard & Elizabeth Longes
Elaine & Bill McLaughlin
Dr Stephen McNamara
Martin Portus
Sue Procter
Pip Rath & Wayne Lonergan
Merilyn Sleigh & Raoul de Ferranti
Mike Thompson
Jane Thorn
Adrian Wiggins & Siobhan Toohill
Paul & Jennifer Winch

Reading Donor $500-$999
Anonymous (4)
Melissa Ball
Angela Bowne
Bernard Coles
Bryony & Tim Cox
Fiona Dewar
Max Dingle
Wendy Elder
Jacqueline Hayes
Michael Hobbs
Susan Hyde
C John Keightley
Daniel Knight
John Lam-Po-Tang
Jennifer Ledgar & Bob Lim
Rebecca Macfarling & Paul Warnes
Lisa Manchur
Carina Martin
John McCallum
Wendy Michaels
Anthony Paull
Alex Oonagh Redmond
Karen Rodgers
& Bill Harris
Diana Simmonds
Catherine Sullivan
Isla Tooth
Judy & Sam Weiss
Simone Whetton
Penny Young

First Draft Donor $200-$499
Anonymous (4)
Priscilla Adey
Jes Andersen
Wendy Ashton
Robyn Ayres
Pamela Bennett
Julie Bridge
Rob Brookman & Verity Laughton
Wendy Buswell
Bryan Cutler
Eric Dole
Susan Donnelly
Tim Duggan
Michele Dulcken
Elizabeth Evatt
Corinne & Bryan Everts

Michael & Kerrie Eyers
Matt Garrett
Sheba Greenberg
Jennifer Hagan
Ross Handsaker
Elizabeth Hanley
Will Harvey & Ester Hardin
John Head
Janet Heffernan
Danielle Hoareau
Mary Holt
Val Jory
Ross Kelly
Carolyn Lowry
Ian & Elizabeth MacDonald
Rob Macfarlan & Nicole Abadee
Stephen Manning
Christopher McCabe
Patrick McIntyre
Duncan McKay
Nicole McKenna
Kent Carrington McPhee
Dr Wendy Michaels
Keith Miller
Sarah Miller
Kate Mulvany
Kerry O'Kane
Annie Page & Colin Fletche
Mario Philippou
Crispin Rice
Rebecca Rocheford Davies
Ellen & Trevor Rodgers
Julie Rosenberg
Catherine Rothery
Dianne & David Russell
Gemma Rygate
Julianne Schultz
Roger Sewell
Jann Skinner
Geoffrey Starr
Augusta Supple
Sue Thomson
Benson Waghorn
Arisa Yura
William Zappa
Aviva Ziegler

We would also like to thank Peter O'Connell for his expertise, guidance and time

Current as of 23/09/2015

GRIFFIN FUND

The Griffin Fund is a new initiative focusing on education programs, leadership pathways for artists, touring Griffin productions and international exchange opportunities. Donations to the Fund are pledged for a three-year period. It is an investment in the future prospects of the company and the artists we work with. For more information please visit griffintheatre.com.au/support-us or contact our Development Manager on 9332 1052.

Founding Donors
Anonymous (1)
Baly Douglas Foundation
John Bell & Anna Volska
Nathan Bennett & Yael Perry
Michael & Charmaine Bradley
Ange Cecco & Melanie Bienemann
Alison Deans & Kevin Powell
Catherine Dovey & Kim Williams
Lilian & Ken Horler
Peter Ingle
Kiong Lee & Richard Funston
Lisa & Ross Lewin
Lee Lewis & Brett Boardman
Sophie McCarthy & Antony Green
Bruce Meagher & Greg Waters
Dr David Nguyen
Peter & Dianne O'Connell
Ian Phipps
Ian Robertson
Will Sheehan
Stuart Thomas
Louise Walsh & Dave Jordan
Simon Wellington & Sanjeev Kumar
Carole & David Yuile

PRODUCTION PATRONS

The Bleeding Tree 2015

Presenting Partner
Gil Appleton

Production Patrons
Peter Brereton
Robert Dick
Richard McHugh & Kate Morgan
Richard Weinstein

Production Partners
Tina & Maurice Green
Jon & Katie King
Bruce Meagher & Greg Waters
John Mitchell
Rachel Procter
Steve Riethoff
Simone Whetton
Carole & David Yuile

GRIFFIN SPONSORS

Griffin would like to thank the following:

Government Supporters

Patron

2016 Season Sponsor

RE:

Production Sponsors

HOLDING REDLICH nabprivatewealth nab

Foundations and Trusts

MALCOLM ROBERTSON FOUNDATION

COPYRIGHTAGENCY CULTURAL FUND

ROBERTSON FOUNDATION

GIRGENSOHN FOUNDATION

Company Lawyers

MAR/QUE

Associate Sponsor

Brett Boardman Photography

Dining Partner

OTTO

Company Sponsors

Time Out Sydney

THE UNIVERSITY OF SYDNEY PERFORMANCE STUDIES

Tatler SYDNEY

bourke street bakery

Rosenfeld, Kant & Co. Business & Financial Solutions

MOPPITY

QUEST Potts Point Serviced Apartments

CURRENCY PRESS

Coopers

FOUR PILLARS SMALL AUSTRALIAN DISTILLERY

Qbt CONSULTING

SIGNWAVE NEWTOWN

Griffin Theatre Company is assisted by the Australian Government through the Australia Council, its arts funding and advisory body; and the NSW Government through Arts NSW.